Aime Cesaire • Alexander Bedward • Aqualtune Filha do Rei do Congo • Arthur Schomburg • Asa Philip Randolph • Bastiaan Karpata • Bayano • Bellaca • Benkos Bioho • Bernie Grant • Biassou • Bishop Henry McNeal Turner • Bob Marley • Bussa • Carlota • Cecile Fatiman • Chatoyer • Chica da Silva • Claudia Jones • C L R James • Cudjoe • Dandara • Dedan Kimathie • Denmark Vessey • Elijah Muhammad • Emperor Haile Selassie • Emperor Menelik II • Eva do Bonsucesso • Eric Williams • Evaristo • Ezili Danto • Fela Anikulapo Kuti • Fermina • Francisco Nascimento • Frantz Fanon • Frederick Douglass • Gabriel Prosser • Gaspar Yanga • General Jean-Jacques Dessalines • General Toussaint L'Ouverture • George Padmore • George William Gordon • Gregorio Luis • Harriet Tubman • Harold Cruse • Henri Christophe • Henrik Clarke • Henry Highland Garnet • High Priest Bookman Dutty • Hubert Harrison • Huey P Newton • Ignatius Sancho • Ira Aldridge • Jean-Francois • Jeannot • Joao de Deus • Joaquin Lezina • Jose Leonardo Chirino • Joseph Chatoyer •

A list of heroes and heroines in the fight against slavery, colonialism, apartheid, segregation and discrimination.

THREE CONTINENTS, ONE HISTORY

Copyright © Individual chapters to their contributors 2008

The right of the individual authors of this work has been identified in accordance with the Copyright, Designs and Patents Act 1988.

Published by Afro-Caribbean Millennium Centre
339 Dudley Road, Winson Green, Birmingham B18 4HB
www.acmccentre.com

British Library Cataloguing-in-Publication Data
A catalogue record for this book is available from the British Library

ISBN 978–0–9559131–0–5

Set in Baskerville and Gill Sans
Designed and produced by Lionart (info@lionart.net)
Printed by Folium Group Ltd, Birmingham
Bound by Hunter & Foulis, Edinburgh

All rights reserved. No part of this publication may be reproduced, stored in a retrieval system, or transmitted, in any form or by any means, electronic, mechanical, photocopying, recording or otherwise, without the prior permission of the publishers.

THREE CONTINENTS, ONE HISTORY:

Birmingham, the Transatlantic Slave Trade and the Caribbean

Clive Harris (ed.)

Afro-Caribbean Millennium Centre
339 Dudley Road, Winson Green, Birmingham B18 4HB
www.threecontinents.co.uk

Sponsors

The Three Continents, One History Project is grateful for the financial support received from its sponsors.

Supported by The National Lottery® through the Heritage Lottery Fund | Heritage Lottery Fund
www.hlf.org.uk

GraceKennedy
www.gracekennedy.com

FIX UP Building Maintenance Limited
Unit 24, 27 Colmore Row, Birmingham B3 2EW
Tel: 0121 551 2057   Fax: 0121 551 9490
fixup@repairman.com   www.fixupltd.co.uk
www.fixupltd.co.uk

Bournville College
www.bournville.ac.uk

WESTERN UNION MONEY TRANSFER
www.westernunion.co.uk

Cover: La maison des esclaves (slave house) with 'Door of No Return' in background, Gorée Island. Courtesy of bdinphoenix, www.flickr.com.

Contents

	Introduction Dr Clive Harris	7
1	**Africa before the Slave Trade** Sophia 'Ankhobia' Carvalho and Dr Clive Harris	10
2	**European Involvement in the Slave Trade** Dr Clive Harris	20
3	**The Middle Passage** Dr Clive Harris	36
4	**Slavery and Emancipation** Dr Clive Harris	44
5	**Resistance** Dr Clive Harris	54
6	**The expression of Africa through Jamaican and Black British Music** Sophia 'Ankhobia' Carvalho	65
7	**Birmingham's manufacturing industries and the European Slave Trade** Dr Clive Harris	74
8	**West Midlands Regiments and the preservation of the Caribbean slave order** Dr Rebecca Condron and Dr Clive Harris	81
9	**Woman to Woman: The Birmingham Female Society for the Relief of British Negro Slaves** Dr Rebecca Condron	90
10	**The Lunar Society in Birmingham and its role in the Abolition of the Slave Trade** Dr Rebecca Condron	94
11	**Black Anti-Slavery Narratives and Transatlantic Identities in Birmingham** Dr Andy Green	102
	Acknowledgements	110

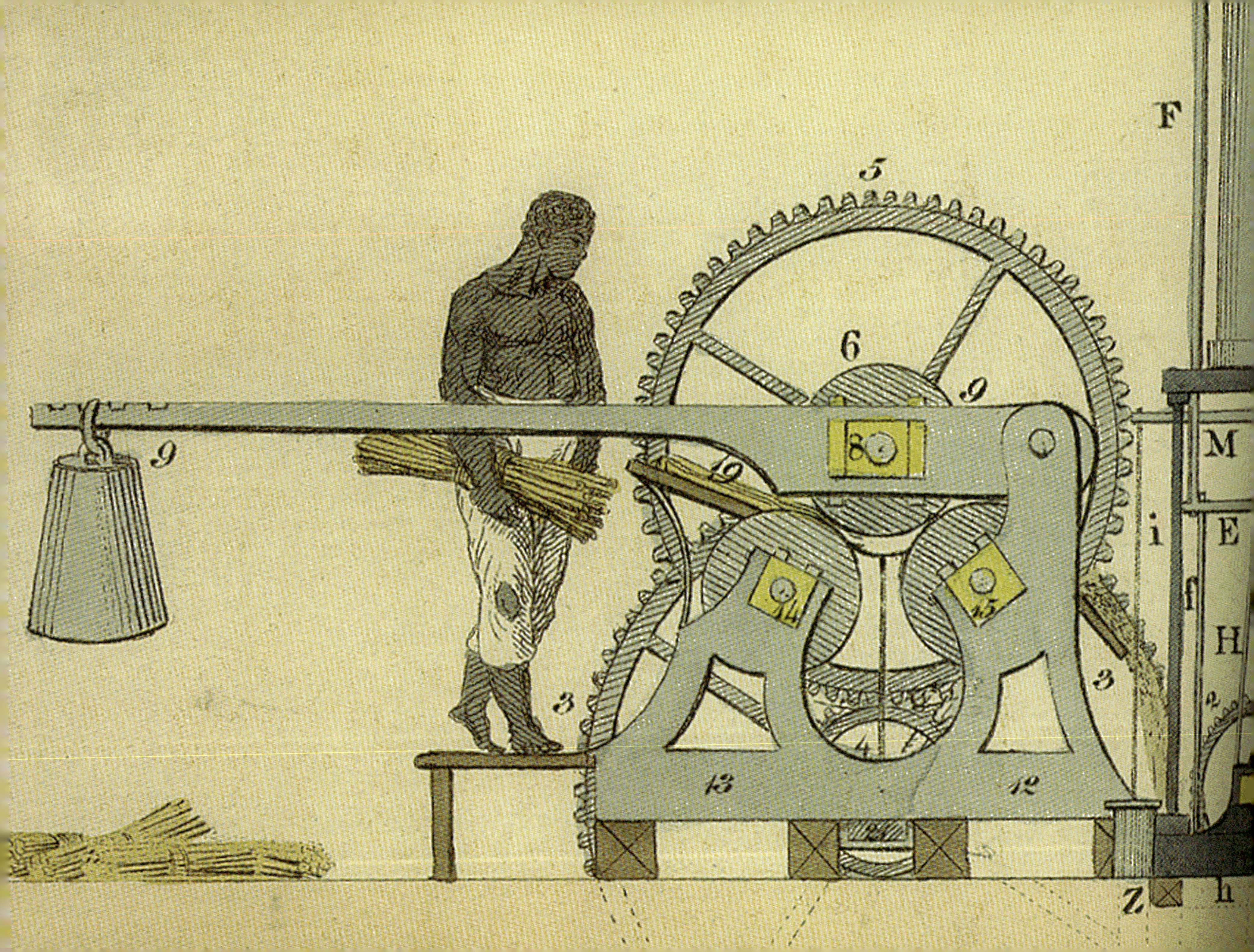

F
5
6
9
9
8
M
10
i
E
14
15
f
H
3
3
2
4
13
12
Z
h

Introduction

In a year in which there has been much endeavour spent in marking the 200th anniversary of the Abolition of the Slave Trade Act by Britain in 1807, the discussion of African history and culture has invariably been reduced to a footnote to the study of slavery and the slave trade and sometimes, more narrowly, to a footnote to the study of abolition. What has often been missing is a systematic and accurate overview of the 447 years of slaving during which Europe sought to bend the will of Africa to that of Europe. Without this overview it seems inconceivable how a debate about legacies can meaningfully take place. In our **Three Continents, One History** Project, we have felt it necessary to deliver a varied programme that places the period of slavery and the slave trade in some historical context. Slavery and the slave trade have been defining moments in the experience of Africans on the continent and in the diaspora, but African history and culture cannot be contained by this experience.

This publication is meant to provide the reader with a sample of the varied topics that our project has addressed over a period of fifteen months. Our weekly Three Continents Radio Shows on New Style Radio 98.7fm., presented by Ankhobia Carvalho and Ebony Matthews, opened quite appropriately with a survey of the various civilisations that have shaped the continent and the region from which the vast majority of enslaved Africans were taken. If this history was well-appreciated and marvelled at by scholars and travellers visiting the region, by the end of the period of European trafficking in Africans, it was as if this Golden Age had never existed. Having plundered the region, and set African against African in a spiral of violence that seemed almost to become an end itself, Europeans now came to see Africans as 'savage' and 'childlike'. Scholars have been reluctant to make the link between the impact of 447 years of trafficking in human beings, the political destabilisation that it entailed, and the fact that no significant regional empire emerged after the downfall of Songhai in 1591.

For Africa, worse was to follow. Having distorted and perverted the course of historical development of African societies, Europe now turned around and said that Africa could only progress by being broken up into different spheres of European influence within which Africans would assume a kind of *statu pupillari*. The workshops and radio shows that the project has put on have tried to get to the heart of this complex history.

Almost every maritime European nation sought to participate in and benefit from a trafficking in Africans

Frontispiece: Model cane crusher designed by Laing & Anderson to enable Boulton & Watt to advertise their steam engine technology to Caribbean planters. Courtesy of Birmingham Archives & Heritage.

that had been given a veneer of legitimacy and acceptability by the various papal bulls passed throughout the fifteenth century by the Vatican. These papal bulls effectively declared war on Africa and proclaimed the capture and enslavement of Africans a religious duty. In the infamous *Illius Qui* document of 1442 enslavement itself was elevated to the status of a crusade which, when performed, allowed the doer to accumulate blessings. Motivated by such ideologies, almost every country that fell on hard times as a result of the prolonged wars and regional conflicts that pervaded the European continent considered it axiomatic that they could recover their fortune by acquiring a few slaving ships, some forts/factories in Africa, and an island or two in the Caribbean region. Chapter 2 gives an insight into the breadth and depth of this European involvement by countries which, today, represent themselves as paragons of human rights.

The deportation and enforced migration across the Atlantic Ocean – the Middle Passage – have in many respects come to symbolise the experiences of millions of Africans. The slaving ship was effectively a carceral regime in which Africans were considered as nothing more than good or bad 'parcels' that could be 'tight packed' like sardines with utter disregard for personal dignity, and subjected to a panoply of technologies of discipline. Violence was wantonly exercised as part of a larger political ordering of life where African life was literally reduced to an insurance statistic. All of these characteristics of the Middle Passage tell us that we are in the presence of an extraordinary event in history, a veritable crime against humanity – a *Maafa* (to use a Swahili word). After 1807, this crime intensified and another million and a half Africans endured the Middle Passage.

The Middle Passage served only to prepare Africans for a plantation and mining regime in the Americas whose sole motive was the making of money/profit. The complex system of domination and discipline that allowed for the extraction of this profit worked on the economic principle that there was no need for the Eupopean planter or mine owner to economise labour. Indeed rational capitalist accounting suggested that it was better to work the African to death and trust to replacements from Africa. If the process was designed to make a 'slave' of the African, it was equally designed to make the European into a 'master'. The legacies of this master/slave relationship are evident today in the pigmentocracy and the circumscribed human rights that exist for people of African descent in the Americas. World Bank statistics reveal that Africans in the New World still experience pervasive discrimination and racialised inequality. In many countries in Latin America, Africans are still trying to take their place as citizens of the countries in which they live and which they helped to build. What this suggests is that the whole emancipation process in each territory of the Americas was a failure. It was designed not to empower Africans and compensate them for their injuries and injustices but to ensure that the economic system introduced by Europeans stayed in place, and continued to work to the advantage of Europe and a small oligarchy in each society.

It must be said though that, despite the social, psychological and sexual domination imposed by Europeans, Africans resisted in varied ways at every stage of the journey from the interior of Africa to the plantation in the Americas. The evidence that is now emerging makes it urgent that we should not allow the complicity of certain strata in African societies in aiding and abetting the trafficking in human beings to overshadow the resistance of ordinary people to a system that placed their own lives in constant danger wherever they lived. In the Americas, Africans sought, where possible, to create spaces inside and outside the plantation system where they could preserve their culture and identity, and fashion a community that provided them with the tools and resources to resist the inhumanity of slavery. In this book, particular attention has been paid to the musical landscape of the Caribbean in allowing us to explore the rich heritage that Africans were able to preserve and recreate. Like music, traditional forms of African religions have provided a central arena for articulating an oppositional politics. This was nowhere more evident than in the Revolt of the Malês in 1835, the Sam Sharpe Christmas Rebellion of 1831-32, and the Haitian Revolution (1791-1804) where Africans struggled for thirteen years against a succession of European armies to free themselves of the incubus of European enslavement.

The heart of our project has been to disclose the threads that have bound the city of Birmingham (UK) to Africa and the Caribbean through the slave trade. The book appropriately references this focus by starting with an examination of the manufacturing connection. The emergence of the city as the premier industrial city of the country was intimately connected with economic links that were forged from the beginning of the eighteenth century. The gun industry has come to symbolise this transformation of the city. Birmingham made and assembled the guns that armed the slave trade by fuelling internecine warfare between African countries. There were companies within the city that specialised in providing the one-stop service necessary for a successful slaving voyage. The fetters and the shackles, the steam engines, the articles of everyday consumption, the decorative ornaments produced in Birmingham ensured that the city benefited from every leg of the Triangular Trade.

The irony is that a number of those whose businesses benefited from the trafficking in Africans appeared also to express support for the Abolitionist cause, gradual abolition that is. Belatedly it fell to women in the city to take a more radical stance on slavery: immediate abolition. In discussions about the contribution of the city to the wider Abolitionist struggle, inadequate attention has been paid to the role played by black residents of and visitors to the city. A section of the book fills this void.

There has never been an empire in history without an accompanying army to defend it. A section of the book explores the particular role that regiments from the West Midlands region, sometimes recruited in Birmingham, played in the preservation of the Caribbean slave order, both by putting down rebellions and in defending the sugar economies of each European country from the predations of other European powers. Particular attention is paid in the book to the Haitian Revolutionary Period when it seemed that conflagration threatened British investment in the Caribbean region.

A key element of the work that we have done has been designed to get us to a position when questions can be posed about the legacies that we wish to leave, and the different ways in which the history addressed by this project can be remembered collectively and individually. We see this as a key challenge that faces us all.

1

Africa before the Slave Trade

Sophia 'Ankhobia' Carvalho and Dr Clive Harris

> 'I am apt to suspect the negroes to be naturally inferior to the whites. There scarcely ever was a civilized nation of that complexion, nor even any individual eminent either in action or speculation. No ingenious manufactures amongst them, no arts, no sciences. On the other hand, the most rude and barbarous of the whites, such as the ancient GERMANS, the present TARTARS, have still something eminent about them, in their valour, form of government, or some other particular. Such a uniform and constant difference could not happen, in so many countries and ages, if nature had not made an original distinction between these breeds of men. Not to mention our colonies, there are NEGROE slaves dispersed all over EUROPE, of whom none ever discovered any symptoms of ingenuity... In JAMAICA, indeed, they talk of one negroe as a man of parts and learning; but it is likely he is admired for slender accomplishments, like a parrot, who speaks a few words plainly.'
>
> David Hume (Scottish philosopher and historian), 'Of national characters', in *Essays: Moral, Political & Literary*, 1741.

Right: Terracotta head from Nok culture (500BC-200AD).

The trafficking in Africans and the imposition of slavery on them was to have a corrosive impact on the European imagination of Africa. Even amongst learned scholars of the European Enlightenment such as David Hume and Georg Hegel who prided themselves on their intellectual rigour and respect for empirical evidence, Africa was transformed into a continent without history and civilisation, a continent of barbarism and childhood, a continent 'enveloped in the mantle of night'. In 1963, the Regius Professor of History at Oxford University, Hugh Trevor Roper, still held to this perverse opinion of Africa: "Perhaps in the future there will be some African history…but at present there is none: There is only the history of the Europeans in Africa. The rest is darkness…. And darkness is not a subject of history." The portrayal of Africa by contemporary news media which conjures up only images of famine, poverty and war, suggests that the task of rescuing Africa from the unashamedly racist and willed ignorance of early scholars remains an uphill task.

This chapter seeks to contribute to this rescue. Not only was Africa the cradle of humanity; it was the location for the emergence of numerous civilisations that made an immense contribution to human development. Our brief survey of these civilisations starts in the Nile Valley with Egypt and Kush (Nubia). From here we proceed south to look at the Axumite Kingdom that arose in Ethiopia/Eritrea. Moving west we come to the Sahel Region of West Africa which was the locus for four of the greatest empires of the continent outside of the Nile Valley. The largest was Ghana, followed by its successor, Mali, and Songhay. To the east in modern day Chad arose a fourth empire which lasted well into the nineteenth century: Kanem-Bornu. These four civilisations represent a veritable Golden Age in West Africa. In the last century, a lot of archaeological evidence has brought to light a spectacular fifth civilisation that existed in the region south of the Jos Plateau area at the confluence of the Niger and Benue Rivers in modern-day Nigeria. This is the Nok culture.

Egypt

Before the emergence of Egypt as the first nation state, there existed what scholars call the Naqada period, a period that was marked by small-scale farming communities and the gradual development of city states. The year 5660 BC is seen as the date when ancient Egypt came into being with the unification of north and south Egypt into a single kingdom – the Old Kingdom – by the first Pharaoh of Egypt, Namer. Memphis was the seat of government. It is during this period of the Old Kingdom that the Great Pyramids were built and the solar calendar was pioneered. Pharaoh Namer established the first of the 32 powerful dynasties that ruled Egypt. Though Egypt went through periods when it was conquered and/or political authority broke down and social chaos and civil war prevailed, the country managed to maintain its unique character even into the period of Greek rule (the Ptolemaic period) which lasted until the death of Cleopatra in 30 BC.

Each period of renewal witnessed the initiation of numerous building projects which have left their mark on the physical landscape of the country. Such was the situation when, after a period of strife, Pharaoh Mentuhotep started the process of reunification that was to lead to the Middle Kingdom. He built not only major forts but also temples. Pharaohs were not just political leaders; they were chief priests. Thebes became the capital of the Middle Kingdom. During the Middle Kingdom period, Lower Nubia ('Wawat') was conquered and made a province of Egypt. Mentuhotep brought great prosperity to the country. Every year the Nile River flooded spreading fertile soil into the desert regions and created an environment where farmers could produce a quantity of crops well beyond their subsistence needs. Mentuhotep sought to maximise the benefit derived from this annual flooding by initiating a number of irrigation and agricultural projects. The Nile River became an important commercial highway that brought goods, culture and people into Egypt from all parts of the ancient world.

The Middle Kingdom period came to an end with the slow invasion of the country by the Hyksos (Hka – Hasaut or 'rulers of foreign countries') from Asia. The Hyksos period was a time of great shame and humiliation for Egypt. When the foreigners were eventually driven out by Pharaoh Ahmose, a New Kingdom (1580-1070 BC) emerged. During Ahmose's reign Egypt re-established control over Nubian territories to the south. The New Kingdom was the Golden Age in which Pharaohs such as Queen Hatshepsut, Amenhotep IV (Akhenaten), Tutankamen and Rameses II made their mark.

The coming to power of Pharaoh Amenhotep IV (Akhenaten) and Queen Nefertiti witnessed a radical attempt to transform Egyptian society by overthrowing the belief in many gods – and the power of the priesthood – in favour of the worship of a single god, Aten, the Sun God. Amenhotep IV changed his name to Akhenaten to symbolise this transformation. A new capital, Amarna, was built. During the reign of the boy king, Tutankamen, Egypt returned to the old religion, and Ahkenaten was declared a heretic. Under Rameses II, who reigned for 66 years (the longest in Egyptian history), the aggressive policy pursued of extending the Egyptian border into Palestine brought Egypt into conflict with powerful enemies such as the Hittites in Anatolia (Turkey). Rameses II was famous as a builder who left behind important monuments at Luxor and Abu Simbel.

Struggles between rival dynasties brought the Middle Kingdom to an end. During the period of turmoil,

> 'Africa proper, as far as History goes back, has remained-for all purposes of connection with the rest of the World-shut up; it is the Gold-land compressed within itself-the land of childhood, which lying beyond the day of history, is enveloped in the dark mantle of Night… At this point we leave Africa, not to mention it again. For it is no historical part of the World; it has no movement or development to exhibit. Historical movements in it-that is in its northern part-belong to the Asiatic or European World. Carthage displayed there an important transitionary phase of civilization; but, as a Phoenician colony, it belongs to Asia. Egypt will be considered in reference to the passage of the human mind from its Eastern to its Western phase, but it does not belong to the African Spirit. What we properly understand by Africa, is the Unhistorical, Undeveloped Spirit, still involved in the conditions of mere nature, and which had to be presented here only as on the threshold of the World's History plainly.'
>
> **Georg Friedrich Hegel (German philosopher),** *The Philosophy of History,* **lectures of 1830-1831.**

THREE CONTINENTS, ONE HISTORY

Kush recovered its autonomy and conquered Egypt using ownership of Jebel Barkal ('Holy Mountain' in Arabic) – the mountain near Napata where the spirit of the creator God, Amun, was said to reside – as providing legitimacy to be the true representative of Egyptian traditions. (Both the ancient Nubians and Egyptians believed that Jebel-Barkal was the site where life on earth began.) Under the new Kushite dynasty of Pharaoh Alara (790-760 BC) Egypt and Kush were united. Kushite rule came to an end when Egypt was invaded by the Assyrians during the reign of Pharaoh Taharka (669 BC). The Assyrians were followed by the Persians who transformed Egypt into a province of the Achaemenid/Persian Empire. Egypt revolted against Persian rule and secured its independence in the fifth century BC under Pharaoh Nekhtnebef II (Nectanebo). Attempts to build support by fomenting strife in Palestine failed, and the Persians re-conquered Egypt. Pharaoh Nekhtnabef was the last Egyptian ruler of Egypt. Persian rule was followed by Greek rule when Alexander the Great conquered Persia and entered Egypt in 332 BC. It is during this period that the library of Alexandria was built. On the death of Cleopatra, the Roman Empire took control of the country.

During Roman occupation Egypt became widely Christianised. After the split in the Roman Empire during the fourth century AD, Egypt became part of the Byzantine Empire with its capital at Constantinople. During the rapid expansion of the Islamic Empire under the second Caliphate of Umar-ibn-al-Khattab, the Byzantine army was defeated in 639 AD at Heliopolis. Under Arab rule, Christianity was gradually replaced by Islam as the state religion; and Egyptian gave way to Arabic as the national language. The succession of foreign invasions leading up to Arab, and later Ottoman, conquest was to have a significant impact on the racial composition of the Egyptian population.

Egyptian contribution to world civilisation has been significant. They produced early forms of paper and had developed a written script based on hieroglyphics before the unification of the country by Pharaoh Namer. Monuments such as the Pyramids of Giza confirmed Egyptian mastery of engineering, and advancement in many other fields such as mathematics, geometry and algebra. Pythogaras's theorem, for example, was known to the ancient Egyptians hundreds of years before Pythogoras's birth. Important Greek scholars such as Archimedes and Pythogoras who studied in Egypt for 21 years, readily acknowledged the debt owed by Greece to Egypt. Egypt also made important contributions to mechanics, philosophy, irrigation and architecture. From the period of the Old Kingdom, Egyptians were also very advanced in medicine, and surviving papyruses – the material used by Egyptians for writing on – demonstrate that they possessed a detailed knowledge of anatomy and the treatment of traumatic surgical lesions.

Kush

The Kingdom of Kush has a history that is intertwined closely with that of its northerly neighbour, Egypt. Recent archaeological evidence at Kerma – the early centre of Kushite settlement – suggests that its history is almost as old, if not older, than Egypt. Kush was the upper (southern) part of the region known as Nubia. Lower Nubia, for a long period of its history, was incorporated into Egypt as the province of Wawat. Today,

Above: Pharaoh Akhenaten, Queen Nefertiti and their children.
Below: Queen Hatshepsut's Mortuary Temple, Deir el-Bahri.

Nubia lies in Sudan. As in Egypt, the Nile was central to the development of the Kushite civilisation. When Egypt went into decline at the end of the 20th Dynasty, the Kingdom of Kush re-emerged as a force centred on its capital at Napata. Kushite culture was heavily inflected with Egyptian influences. Gradually, the kingdom extended its borders northwards. Under the leadership of Piankhy, Egypt was conquered and the two states were unified. Thus began the XXV Dynasty of Kushite Pharaohs such as Alara, Kashta, Shabaka and Taharka. During the reign of Taharka, Egypt was invaded by the Assyrians, and the Kushites were forced to retreat up the Nile. When the old Kushite capital of Napata was captured, administration was transferred to the new capital at Meroë.

The Kushites were famous for their impressive architecture, irrigation systems, scripts and iron industry. Learning from their defeat in Egypt at the hands of the Assyrians when their bronze weapons were no match for the iron weapons of the Assyrians, Kush began mining iron ore deposits and learned to smelt iron. Meroë became the centre of trade routes from the interior of Africa to Egypt, the Middle East and Asia more generally for commodities such as iron, gold and ivory. Unlike Egypt, Kushite kings derived their position from a customary law in which the influence of priests was strong. Kings were elected from within the royal family. Descent through the maternal line produced a series of powerful female queens such as Amanirenas, Amanishakheto and Amanitore – a fact which happened only rarely in Egypt. Royal tombs in Kush were pyramid-shaped, though smaller and steeper. Today more pyramids can be found in Kush than in Egypt. As Meroë became more isolated from Egyptian influences during Egypt's occupation by foreigners, Kush adopted a 23-symbol alphabet to replace Egyptian hieroglyphics. Literacy was high in Kush. Religious practices were modelled on the Egyptian lines, though with the addition of the Kushite god, Apedemak. The period 90 BC – 1 AD marks the height of the Meroitic civilisation. From 200 AD, Kush went into a period of decline and was eventually overrun by the Axum Empire in 350 AD.

Above: 'Pyramiden von Meroë' (Sudan, remains of a royal cemetery from the Meroitic kingdom (between 300 BC and 300 AD), published in Meyer's Universum ..., 1838.
Below: Stele (obelisk) of Negus Ehanza, hewn from a single granite rock 4th century AD.

Axum

Axum was both a city and an empire located in the highlands of northern Ethiopia/Eritrea close to the Red Sea. Scholars generally date the start of the Axumite Kingdom around 200 BC. By the 1st century AD, Adulis had become the principal port city that connected the Axum Empire to trade routes along the Red Sea and Indian Ocean with Rome, Greece, Arabia and India. Between the second and fourth centuries AD, Axum controlled most of Ethiopia/Eritrea, and territories in the Arabian peninsula. In 350 AD they conquered Kush. In the 3rd century the Persian writer, Manni, listed Axum as one of the four great kingdoms of the world along with Persia, China and Rome.

After his conversion to Christianity, King (Negus) Ehanza, made Christianity the state religion in 329 AD. In 372 AD the great church of St Mary of Zion was built supposedly to house the Arc of the Covenant. During the fifth century AD, the Axumites replaced Greek in the liturgy and began using their own native language, Ge'ez.

Above: Ge,ez script.
Below: Bet Giorgis (St. George's): one of the twelve rock-hewn churches in Lalibela, Ethiopia, 13th century.

Axum remained a strong empire and trading power until the decline of the Byzantine and Persian Empires and the expansion of the second Islamic Caliphate in the seventh century. As the Islamic Caliphate spread, the trade routes changed leaving Axum isolated commercially. Because of the sanctuary that the Negus Armah had accorded to Muslim refugees fleeing from persecution in Arabia in 615 AD, including members of Prophet Mohammed's family, the Prophet instructed his followers to leave the country alone and exempt it from jihad: "Leave the Abyssinians alone, so long as they do not take the offensive!" This perhaps explains why Axum/Ethiopia managed to survive as a Christian country when Christian countries around it such as Egypt and Nubia fell to Islam.

Little is known of the history of Axum between the eighth and eleventh centuries. Around the middle of the eleventh century, Axum transformed itself into the Ethiopian state under the Zagwe dynasty. Zagwe rule lasted until the thirteenth century when the old Axumite dynasty reasserted itself. The brilliant achievement of the Zagwe dynasty was the construction of a dozen wonderful churches hewn from sandstone rock at Roha/Lalibela by Prince Lalibela who reigned from 1167 to 1207.

NOK Culture

One of the earliest civilisations in West Africa which left behind some astonishingly sophisticated artefacts is the culture of the Nok. Scholars do not know what the people who created this civilisation called themselves. The term Nok is the name of the town in the Jos Plateau area of Nigeria, at the confluence of the Niger and Benue Rivers, where the artefacts of this ancient culture have been unearthed. The culture flourished between 900 and 500 years BC and lasted until around 200 AD. Cultures never really disappear, and it is said that there are many artistic similarities between early Yoruba art forms and Nok forms.

Whereas most ancient cultures discovered copper and bronze before iron, the Nok seemed to jump from the Stone Age to the Iron Age. The malleability of iron meant that it could be shaped into weapons and ploughs. Nok culture is best known, however, not for its iron ware, but its terracotta figures. Nok culture produced some of the oldest sculpture in West Africa, made from fired clay or terracotta. The sculpted figures tend to be adorned with elaborately designed hairstyles and jewellery, and reveal a strong devotion to beauty and body ornamentation.

Ghana (700 – 1076 AD)

Imagine this: Homes built out of stone with glass windows with an upstairs and downstairs floor, sculptures and pictures on walls, princes with hair plaited with gold, dogs wearing collars of silver and gold. This is a description of the Kingdom of Ancient Ghana (Wagadu), or the 'the land of gold' as it was called. As Islam swept across North Africa, the Soninke people united around 700 AD to form the first great empire in West Africa. The Soninke, a Mande speaking people, were rich in culture, spirit, and wealth. The name Ghana actually means king, but the kingship was matrilineal, i.e. the lineage of the royal family was traced through the female line and not the male. Old Ghana was in a different location to modern Ghana. The former was located in today's Mali, southern Mauritania and parts of Senegal and Guinea. The Ghana Empire was at its most powerful during the eleventh century. Its capital, Kumbi-Saleh, was an important political and economic centre.

Ghana's wealth was based on international trade. The government taxed imports and exports of goods, making the Treasury very rich. Ghana also produced and traded metal goods, cotton cloth and copper. They sold their high quality leather to Moroccans who then sold it on to Europeans as 'Moroccan leather'. Cheques were an accepted method of payment in tenth century Ghana. An Arab geographer visiting Ghana in the tenth century wrote about his amazement at seeing the amount of money in circulation in the region. He talked about a cheque for 42,000 golden dinars, written to a merchant by his business partner!

Descriptions of Ghana's city life portray the king as living in a castle and domed buildings surrounded by walls. There was a royal court of justice, with lawyers and scholars. The capital city was "the resort of the learned, the rich, and the pious of all nations". Every morning the emperor would ride out on well dressed horses around the poorest cities, accompanied by his entire court. Any one who had a grievance could address him and he would administer justice. No one would move from his presence until the matter had been resolved. Even the lowliest person could speak to the king.

In 1007 AD, the great nation state of ancient Ghana began to fall apart. The Almoravids, a veil-wearing, hard-line Islamic movement from Morocco posed the first serious threat to the power of Ghana. They despised Ghanaian rule. By 1055 the Almoravids took Audoghast and Tekrur from Ghanaian rule. In 1076, they declared another holy war on Ghana and ransacked its capital. A large part of northern Ghana was converted to Islam. Almoravid rule over the empire did not last long, and collapsed within ten years. Things, however, would never be the same; the ancient glory had gone.

As the Ghana Empire fell apart, it gave rise to new independent kingdoms such as Mali and Tekrur. In 1180 some Soninkes established a rival kingdom in southern Ghana. The Sosso, also Ghanaians, launched raids on the capital in the early thirteenth century and began to attack the country of Mali. The Sosso were anti-Muslim and resented attempts to forcibly convert them to Islam. The rise of Mali would eventually lead to the fall of Sosso and Ghana. This would end a glorious era in history. However ancient Ghana's legacy would live on.

Mali or Manding Empire (1235-1550)

The popular statement, 'From here to Timbuktu' conjures up images of remote and distant parts of the planet, a fantasy place that does not exist. Well, Timbuktu does exist, and it was part of the ancient civilisation of the Mali or Manding Empire. As Mali emerged into prominence from the ruins of ancient Ghana, it faced problems from rival powers. In 1224 the Sosso raided the Malian capital, burnt the city, and killed most of the ruling family except one prince, a crippled boy called Sundiata (Sun-JAH-tuh). The Sossos perceived that he would never be a threat to them, and thought that he could be used as a puppet. They were wrong! Six years later, despite his disability, Sundiata triumphed and became the ruler of the Mali Empire. He swore he would one day avenge the wrong done to his family. The lion prince began a guerrilla campaign against the Sosso's dominance and defeated

Above: Bet Giorgis (St. George's): one of the twelve rock-hewn churches in Lalibela, Ethiopia, 13th century.
Below: Map of West African empires.

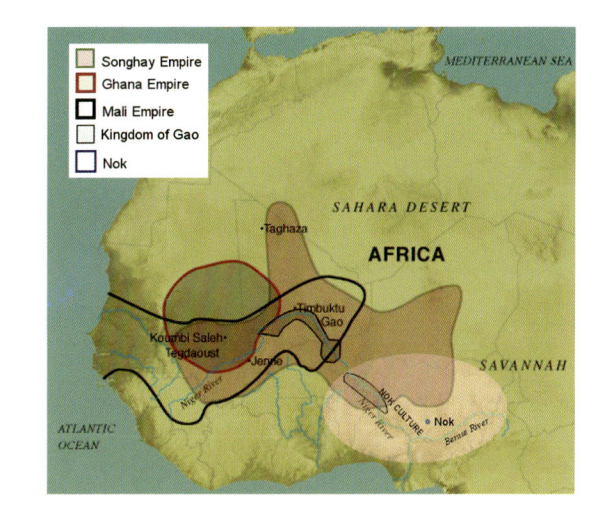

Right: 1375 Catalan map of Africa and Europe depicting *Mansa Musa* holding a gold nugget.

> 'Much alluvial gold was panned but most of the ore was obtained by sinking shafts sometimes 100 ft deep, often linked by side shafts and galleries. It is estimated that the total amount of gold mined in West Africa up to 1500 was 3,500 tons, worth more than $30 billion in today's market.'
>
> **Dr Charles Finch in 1998**

them in 1235. This date is taken as the starting point of the Mali or Manding Empire. The social order of Mali was based along matrilineal lines. Ibn Battuta, an acclaimed traveller, described the women as "extremely beautiful and more important than the men".

Five years after defeating the Sossos, Sundiata seized the city of Kumbi-Saleh and gained control over the gold and salt trade, and eventually over the copper mines. The three immense gold mines provided immense wealth to the Empire. At the time, Mali produced over half of the Old World's gold.

At the height of its power, in the fourteenth century, Mali extended its borders over a region roughly the size of Western Europe. It included the countries that today we call Senegal, Gambia, Mauritania and Niger. Many people tend to think of Mali solely as a Muslim state, and begin its history with its first Muslim king. Mali was however a kingdom for two hundred and fifty years before Islam was adopted as the state religion.

Sundiata founded a new capital called Niani. He may have been Mali's greatest emperor but he was perceived as a poor Muslim, since he practiced Islam alongside his traditional African religion. When he died he was buried in a traditional African step pyramid.

In 1310 *Mansa* Musa succeeded Abubakar II as ruler. Musa told a Syrian scholar that he had become ruler because Abubakar II had left the country on an expedition across the Atlantic Ocean with 2,000 ships – 1,000 for him and his men and 1,000 for provisions. The chronicle states that, before this trip, Abubakar had first sent one hundred ship filled with two years' worth of supplies across the Atlantic Ocean. Eventually one ship came back. Abubakar then decided to explore the Americas for himself. He was never seen again. His Atlantic voyage happened 181 years before Christopher Columbus 'discovered' the Americas. Columbus himself reported that he had acquired metal goods of West African manufacture from the Native Americans. How did West African goods get to America before Columbus arrived? Old maps drawn by Europeans also show that the Malians renamed places in Mexico after themselves: Mandinga Port, Mandinga Bay and Sierre de Mali. In the Dutch Virgin Islands skeletons of two African males were found dated at 1250 (just 61 years away from the proposed Malian visit). Not far from this location an old inscription was discovered that read "Plunge in to cleanse yourself. This is water for purification before prayer".

Mansa Musa is most famous for his pilgrimage across the Sahara to Mecca in 1324. His entourage was of a size unheard of before: 60,000 men. In his entourage he had a personal retinue of 12,000 slaves, all dressed in brocade and Persian silk. *Mansa* Musa himself rode on horseback, and directly preceding him were 500 slaves, each carrying a staff of gold weighing about six pounds. Then came *Mansa* Musa's baggage train of eighty camels, each carrying 300 pounds weight of gold dust. *Mansa* Musa's piety, generosity, fine clothes and the good behaviour of his followers, all quickly made a good impression. When he passed through Egypt, he spent so much money in gold that he devalued Egypt's economy for several years.

Mali became famous for its wealth and learning. To manage the different ethnic groups that made up the population, the Empire adopted a federal structure based on a system of laws that unified the different groups and kingdoms. The most famous city of Mali was Timbuktu, one of the foremost centres of Islamic scholarship in the world. Under the leadership of *Mansa* Musa, a large programme of building mosques and universities was commenced. The university of Sankore Mosque was highly distinguished for the teaching of Koranic theology, law and other subjects such as astronomy and mathematics. According to Professor Louis Henry Gates, 25,000 students studied in these universities. Arab scholars longed for the opportunity to teach in Timbuktu. So when *Mansa* Musa made his way back from Mecca he brought with him some of the top Arab scholars. To his great surprise, the Emperor found that these scholars were under-qualified compared to the African scholars of Timbuktu. They were not allowed to teach at the universities until they had received further training.

Mansa Musu died in 1337. Today the Mandinka people are spread throughout a number of African countries: Guinea, Gambia, Senegal, Ivory Coast, Burkina Faso and Guinea-Bissau. Storytelling by their griots is still an important part of their culture to remind them of their place in history.

Timbuktu

'There are many judges, doctors and clerics here, all receiving good salaries from King Askia Mohammed of the State of Songhay. He pays great respect to men of learning. There is a great demand for books, and more profit is made from the trade in books than from any other line of business.'

Leo Africanus, 16th century.

Kanem-Bornu (1200-1893)

To the east of Mali, in what today is Chad, another empire emerged almost the same time as the Manding Empire. This was the Kanem-Bornu Empire of the Kanuri people which was founded in 1200 and lasted until the European Scramble for Africa in 1893. Some scholars locate the emergence of the Kanem half of Kanem-Bornu back in the ninth century. The Bornu Empire was to continue the dynasty of the Kanem state in what is modern-day Niger. The Kanem Empire originated on the north-east side of Lake Chad. Its expansion peaked in the middle of the thirteenth century under the long reign of *Mai* Dunama Dabbalemi. As a convert to Islam, he sought to destroy Kanuri traditional religion by waging a jihad, or 'holy war' against surrounding chieftaincies. This precipitated one of the most dynamic periods of conquest in Africa. At the height of the empire, the Kanuri controlled territory from Libya to Lake Chad to Huasaland. In the late fourteenth century, internal strife weakened the empire and led to a shift of Kanuri power from Njimi to Bornu on the western edge of Lake Chad. With the fall of the Songhai Empire the Bornu Empire grew rapidly and reached its peak under *Mai* Idris Aluma (1571-1603). The Empire would last for another 200 years before it lost significant territory to the rising power of the Hausa states in the nineteenth century.

Songhai (690-1591)

The Songhai people are thought to have settled at Gao in what is now Niger and Burkino Faso between the seventh and ninth century. The first Songhai dynasty, the Dia, ruled from 690 AD until 1335. Kukya was their capital city. The fifteenth ruler of Kukya, moved the capital to Gao in the early eleventh century joining the two kingdoms. By the time Songhai got it first Islamic King in 1009, Songhai was already 320 years old. Gao was divided into two main sections based on religion, just like the old Ghanaian capital, Kumbi-Saleh, which was split between Traditional religion and Islam.

After the demise of the Mali Empire, Gao, under the leadership of Sonni Suleiman Ber, rose to become the centre of the new Songhay empire. His first notable achievement was the capture of the city of Timbuktu in 1469 and the city of Djenne in 1473. Sonni knew he had to unite his Empire, which was composed of Islamic people and those who kept their traditional African beliefs. He went as far as to adopt a Muslim name himself, in an attempt to placate Africans who had become followers of Islam.

Sonni Ali Ber established the Songhai state as a great regional empire. He became a world famous leader in his time, annexing most of the Malian Empire and establishing an effective centralised system of government. Sonni Ali was a planner and a fearless conqueror. He developed the army, administration, agriculture, irrigation techniques and tax controls. Killed in a military campaign in November 1492, he never gave up his traditional Songhai religion, and did not recognise Islam as the state religion. He was mummified according to very ancient African traditions.

His son replaced him but refused all attempts to convert to Islam. After several weeks of negotiations and no conversion, the Muslims resorted to battle. Backed by a large section of the army in 1493, they triumphed.

Great Mosque of Djenne. Djenne emerged as a major trading city around 800 AD, and as an important centre of learning after the conversion of the city to Islam – symbolised by the building of the mosque in 1220 by Koi Kanburo. The current building dates from 1907. It is made of sun-baked mud bricks ('ferey'). Its conical spires represent the spirits of the ancestors. The palm wood embedded in the walls provide structural support and serve as scaffolding during the annual repair of the mud bricks.

This brought Mohammed Toure, a former general, to power. Such was his international reputation that the Caliph of Egypt (the Pope of the Islamic church) appointed him as his religious representative in West Africa, making him the spiritual leader of all West African Muslims. Ultimately, Songhai would cover an area the size of Europe.

Mohammed Toure's feats were to earn him the title 'Askia The Great'. He established a central government. Amongst the most important posts were the Minister of Treasury, the Minister of Tax Collection, the Minster of the Army and Navy, and the Minister of Trade and Industry. In addition, he strongly encouraged high educational standards. This resulted in an educational system that had an international reputation for excellence. In 1529 Askia The Great was deposed by his son, Musa, and confined to an island of locusts. He died in 1538 and, like Sonni Ali Ber, was buried in a step pyramid at Gao. The pyramid can still be seen today.

To the north, in Morocco, the eunuch Al Mansur began to conspire against Songhai. In 1577 he began seeking alliances to help build his kingdom. He found a ready ally in Queen Elizabeth I of England. Concerned about the threat posed by Spain, an enemy of Morocco, she secretly negotiated to supply Morocco with timber, artillery, cannonballs, guns and soldiers to help build Morocco's navy in the hope that this force would be used against Spain. Al Mansur was much more interested in the gold of prosperous Songhai. After 13 years of planning he invaded Songhai. Although Songhai scouts were able to raise the alarm and give the war council time to prepare to do battle with their superior numbers, Al Mansur had the upper hand in the form of guns, ammunition and canons that the English had sold him. Songhai had none of these weapons and many lost their lives. Al Mansur ransacked, pillaged and burnt to the ground the cities of Djenne, Gao and Timbuktu. His army filled in water wells and destroyed the field crops. The contrasting situation of the two countries after the invasion is extremely well captured by two historians of the period.

Al Mansur became ill and was replaced by another eunuch Mahmud Ben Zergun. Mahmud led his troops to commit many brutal acts. One of these was the capture of Sankore University professors. The arrests took place in October 1593. The captured scholars were deported to Morocco in chains, some were killed on the journey, others were forced to serve the Moroccans or jailed. The head of the University, Professor Ahmed Baba lost 1600 books in this way. Other scholars with even larger libraries lost even more books.

The fall of Songhai in 1591, coming as it did when Europeans were encroaching from the Atlantic seaboard, was bad news for West Africa. The political vacuum and instability created by the emergence of small warring states was to provide conditions that were ripe for an intense period of slaving activity at the hands of Arab missionaries and European traders.

Morocco

'[Al Mansur] received so much gold-dust, musk, slaves, ebony, and other valuable objects, says the [Moroccan] chronicle, "that the envious are troubled and all spectators are stupefied. He now pays his functionaries in pure metal of good weight." From which it would appear that he had not been above falsifying his coinage. "There were fourteen [hundred] smiths in his palace employed in making the gold into coins, while other portions of the treasure were converted into necklaces and jewels, and the name of 'the Golden' was given to the sultan." Great public rejoicings continued at Marrakesh during three days, and deputations came from all parts to offer congratulations'.

Songhai

'The high cost of food … was excessive, a great number of people died from hunger and the famine was such that people ate the corpses of draft animals and of human beings. The exchange rate fell to 500 cowries. Then the plague came in turn to decimate the population and killed many that the famine had spared. The high cost of food, which lasted two years, ruined the inhabitants, who were reduced to selling their furniture and utensils. All the elders were unanimous in saying that they had never seen such a calamity and that not one of the elders before then had ever told them about anything like it.'

As-Sadi, 17th century Songhai historian.

> *At the Palace, Potsdam, Brandenburg*
> *To: Hon. Pregate Sophonie Apany*
>
> You, most Honourable and Noble Cabissiers on the Guinea-Gold Coast, between Axim and Cape Three Points.
> Our beloved friends,
> We have learnt how some of our sea officers sent by us to Guinea, having reached your coast under the providence and guidance of the Most High, made a treaty with you on the 16th May in this year 1681, in which you bound yourselves not to trade with anyone, whoever he may be, but with our ships and people and to bring the surrounding places with you into similar arrangement and that you pointed out to our aforesaid officers a place where a fort could be built and also accepted as your protecting lord.
> As this has been welcomed and agreeable to us to hear therefore, we have readily and willingly approved the afore said treaty and endowed a certain person with authority to ratify same on our behalf. We sent also all that is required not only for the building of such a fort but also the defense of the same as also the gift promised and in addition to those, more again, that you may thereby the better know our graciousness.
> We also, then herewith take you also under our protection and command, our servants to protect you against your enemies to the utmost of our powers.
>
> Given to our Palace of Potstam, the 6th of May 1681.
> Signed
> His Serene Highness Fredrick Williams I
>
> **(Letter, dated 16th May 1681, by the Great Elector of Brandenburg to the chiefs and people of Prince's Town.)**

2

European involvement in the Slave Trade

Dr Clive Harris

When we talk about the European enslavement of Africans we are talking about an economic, political and social relationship that linked three continents: Europe, Africa, and the Americas. From a European perspective, the transatlantic slave trade represented an important turning point; it generated wealth for industrial expansion. From an African perspective, the slave trade and slavery – spanning four centuries – was nothing less than the underdevelopment of the continent. Worse, it was a crime against humanity that can be deemed to merit the term Holocaust or Maafa – the Kiswahili term for 'an event of great disaster, calamity or terrible occurrence'.

The first method by which Europeans sought to acquire Africans as labourers for their New World plantations and mines was through straightforward abduction/kidnapping. Ships anchored at random places along the African coast in order to engage in man-hunts. This was a risky business as evidenced by the massacre of all members of a Portuguese slaving expedition in 1446 in present-day Senegal. Slave-raiding could never guarantee the supply needed to fuel an expanding plantation market. Europeans therefore moved swiftly from seizing Africans to trafficking in Africans through the medium of local merchants and leaders.

European governments sought to regulate the trafficking by according a franchise to various national companies established under royal decree or parliamentary order. In many cases the king was a major shareholder. One of the first regulatory acts of such companies was to build a string of forts/trading centres/slave factories along the West African coast. In Ghana alone there were 60 such forts. In many of these forts, a military presence was maintained to enforce the trade agreement with local leaders and to protect the trafficking from the predation of competitors and other adventurers.

Though some African leaders saw in the alliances with Europeans an opportunity to acquire wealth and expand the power and influence of their kingdoms, for many others the message was simple: participate or perish; sell someone else or be sold. To increase the volume of individuals who could be bought, Europeans provided a steady flow of rifles, ammunition and gunpowder to fuel internecine wars between African states where the assured outcome was a steady stream of prisoners/captives. Sometimes they would themselves enter a local conflict in support of one group or another. When a 'slackness' in the African market prevailed, this was attributed to a lack of war, and hence captives. Whatever the benefit derived by local rulers, Europe dominated the relationship; they shaped and promoted the trafficking, and ensured that the outcome was to the advantage of Europe from first to last.

The transatlantic trafficking was to have massive impact on the three continents that it touched. For Africa and Africans, it represented the most extensive forced migration of human beings in history. It is estimated that between 1450 and 1870, some 15-20 million able-bodied and productive Africans were removed from local economies and transported across the Atlantic. This figure excludes the millions who died during the voyage – the Middle Passage – and those who died from the moment of capture and arrival at the European slaving factories dotted along the African coast. To date, scholars have documented over 30,000 voyages made by slaving ships from Africa to the Americas.

In the Caribbean, Africans were used to replace a Native American population that had been decimated by hard labour, disease and outright genocide at the hands of Europeans. In the region, an almost constant state of war prevailed between European nations competing to secure benefit from the slave trade and the valuable output from the plantations developed in Caribbean territories. Islands were frequently attacked by hostile forces which sometimes conquered the entire island and/or carried off significant numbers of enslaved Africans.

Within Europe, the profits from the New World plantations and from the trafficking in Africans itself produced unimaginable wealth for individuals, companies and countries. The investment of these profits transformed the urban and rural fabric of European societies. In Britain, profits from the trafficking spread across the face of the country, from stately homes to grand London residences, from textile factories to gunmakers and shipbuilders; from mercantile houses to banking and insurance companies. From the middle of the seventeenth century the tastes and habits of both rich and working people were transformed by the consumption of the staples produced by enslaved Africans: sugar, tobacco, coffee, and so on. As owners of plantations retired to Europe to enjoy their newfound wealth, and seek a social position to go with it, they brought with them a retinue of enslaved African servants whose very presence – in their country and town houses and at the watering holes for the rich – was meant to symbolise that wealth. At watering holes such as Lichfield, slave markets were a not uncommon sight.

A lasting legacy of the trafficking in Africans – reflected in the euphemistic ways in which traders spoke about the crime against humanity in which they were engaged as 'the matter', and Africans who were too old or too young as 'bad parcels' – was a complex set of racialised and sexualised attitudes and discourses which elevated white Europeans to the pinnacle of a presumed Chain/Ladder of Being and denigrated Africans to the lowest rung with animals.

Trans-Atlantic 'Triangular' Slave Trade route transporting firearms, salt cloth etc. from Britain to the west coast of Africa. Captured Africans transported as 'cargo' across to the West Indies and North America. Ships picked up rum and sugar for the return leg to Britain.

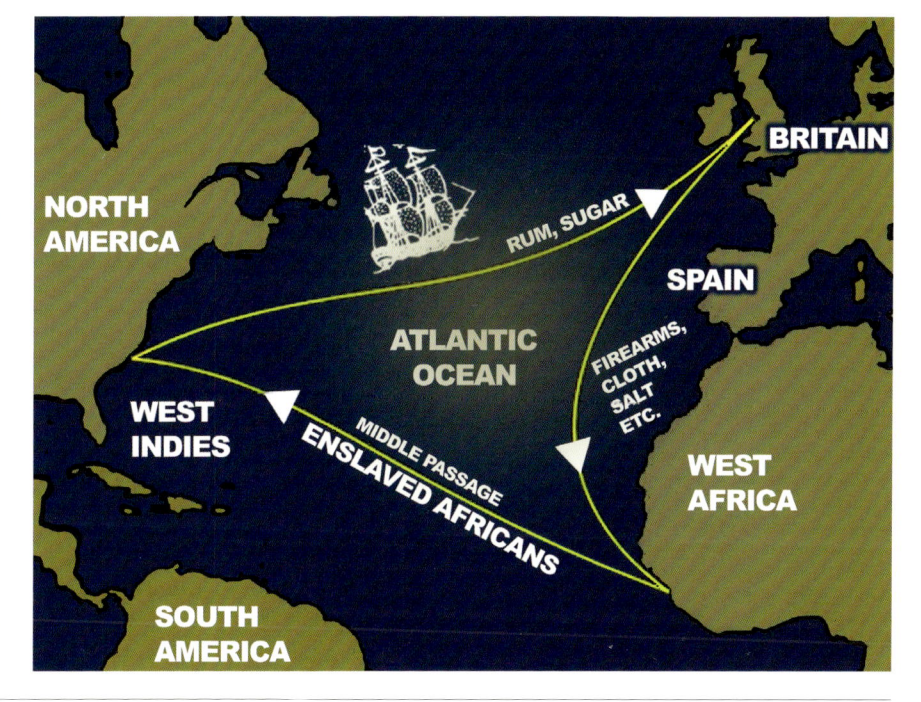

Right: Imaginary line of longitude dividing world into Spanish and Portugese zones imposed by Pope Alexander VI.
Below: Diamond washing, Serro Frio, Brazil, ca. 1770s. Source: Carlos Juliano, *Riscos illuminados de figurinhos de broncos e negras dos uzos do Rio de Janeiro Serro do Frio*. Copyright © 2000, 2001, 2002 Free Software Foundation, Inc.

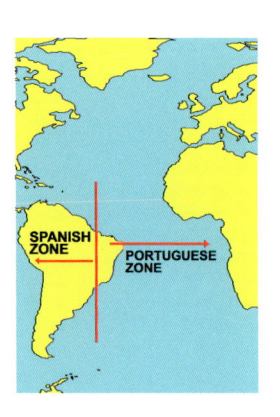

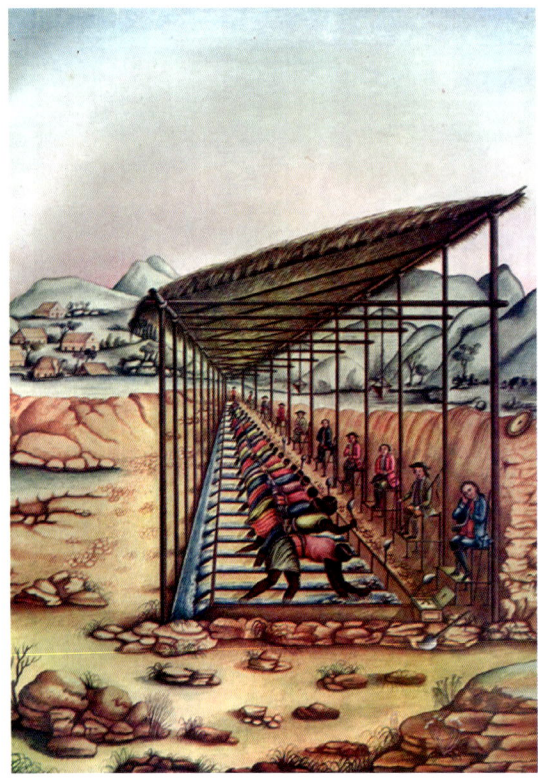

COUNTRIES INVOLVED IN THE TRAFFICKING

The trafficking in Africans was a truly European project that involved virtual every country which had a maritime presence: Portugal, Spain, Netherlands, United Kingdom, France, Sweden, Denmark-Norway, Brandenburg-Prussia (Germany), Duchy of Courland (Latvia), and even landlocked Switzerland.

PORTUGAL

The first Europeans to arrive on the coast of West Africa were the Portuguese in 1441. They came in search of gold, not enslaved Africans. Ever since the pilgrimage to Mecca by *Mansa* Musa, the region had become fabled for its gold. The only problem for the Portuguese was that the gold trade was controlled by the Islamic empire in northern Africa. The solution was to develop new routes by going south to tap into the Saharan gold trade. This the Portuguese achieved by establishing a base at Elmina ('the mine") in modern-day Ghana. Slavery had been endemic in the Iberian Peninsula since the time of the Roman Empire. The initial trafficking in Africans that developed started not as transatlantic trafficking but as old-world trafficking supplying the slave markets of Lisbon and thence onwards to Spain and Italy. This trafficking was legitimised by the papal bulls of the 1452 and 1455 – *Dum Diversas* and *Romanus Pontifex* – which gave the Portuguese King, Afonso V, the right to reduce to "perpetual slavery" all "Saracens and pagans and other infidels and enemies of Christ" in West Africa. Competition from Spain led to conflict between the two countries which Pope Alexander VI was called upon to adjudicate. Under the Treaty of Tordesillas (1494), the Pope imposed an imaginary line of longitude to divide the world into East and West. Portugal was accorded dominion over West Africa (and Brazil); Spain was given dominion over the Americas minus Brazil.

What transformed the primarily domestic use of enslaved Africans in Portugal was the establishment of bases in the islands off the coast of Africa – Madeiras, Cape Verde and Sao Tome – at the end of the fifteenth century. The growing of sugar cane in the islands required a labour force that only Africa was perceived as offering a permanent solution to. From being stopping-off points on the way to Lisbon, the islands soon became centres for the development of sugar cultivation. The development of Brazil as a sugar and mineral colony from the 1530s onwards fuelled the expansion of Portuguese involvement in trafficking. The increased demand for African labour was to change radically the relationship between Portugal and the African states such as the Kongo with which it had developed trading relations.

To protect its trafficking, Portugal built forts along the African coast. From their initial bases on the island of Arguin, Elmina and Sao Tome, they moved further south to set up a trading post at Gwato (Benin), and San Salvador (Kongo). As their involvement in the trafficking grew, they often leased the right to establish posts to individuals and companies that were able to ally themselves with local leaders in order to exchange goods for captured Africans.

Until the beginning of the seventeenth century, the trafficking in Africans was primarily a Portuguese affair. The virtual annexation of Portugal by Spain from 1580 to 1640 only served to tighten the Portuguese grip on the trafficking. In line with the Treaty of Tordesillas, Phillip II granted Portuguese merchants a monopoly on the importation of Africans into the Spanish colonies in the Americas. By renting the Spanish asiento – the contract to supply Africans to the Spanish American colonies – and having secure control over the coast of West Africa by royal monopolies, Portuguese merchants managed simultaneously to control the major supplying and consumption markets for Africans. Before 1650, the Portuguese transported more than 95 percent of the Africans trafficked.

The delinking of Portugal from Spain in 1640 provided an opportunity for countries such as England and the Netherlands to challenge and break Portuguese monopoly of the trafficking in Africans, initially by looting Portuguese ships, and latterly by taking over Portuguese forts on the African coast. With the loss of Elmina to the Dutch in 1637, the Portuguese were forced to go further south towards Angola. It was principally from this location that they sought to supply a rapacious Brazilian market.

Supply was always short of demand, and the Portuguese were forced to buy from their competitors. The loss of the Brazilian market after the country declared its independence in 1822 deprived Portugal of its main source of wealth. It did not however prevent Portuguese merchants from trafficking in Africans despite having reluctantly signed the 1817 Vienna Convention outlawing the slave trade. Instead, they took advantage of the various loopholes in the legislation to expand their business, sometimes acquiring fake papers and flags, or using dual passports that enabled them to simultaneously trade south and north of the Equator – a defining line in early slave trade abolition conventions.

Though Portugal's former colony, Brazil, agreed in 1826 to end the slave trade in 1830, 1825-30 was a boom period in the trafficking in Africans. 1830 came and went without any noticeable decrease in the trafficking; and in the 1840s Brazil imported approximately 340,000 Africans. The volume trafficked in 1848 – 60,000 – reached levels that were comparable to the British endeavours of the late eighteenth century. In 1850, Brazil finally decided to make trafficking an act of piracy. Illegal trafficking and the system of slavery did not actually cease in Brazil until as late as 1888. The Portuguese were the first European country to enter the trafficking; they were the last to abolish it. It is estimated that during the four and a half centuries of their transatlantic trafficking in Africans, the Portuguese were responsible for transporting over 4.5 million Africans.

Engraving (detail) of Elmina Castle, Ghana, during the era of Portuguese control. Source: O. Dapper (1670/1976) *Beschreibung von Afrika*.

SPAIN

Despite the extensive nature of its colonial possessions in the Americas, Spain's involvement in the transatlantic slave trade has been unusual. The long history of slavery in the Iberian peninsular, going back to Roman times, and sustained during the 700 years of Arab conquest and domination, had led to the early codification of a regulatory system of 'slave laws' in 1265, known as the *Siete Partidas*. There was therefore little opposition to a similar use of Africans in the New World context after the early decimation of Native Americans.

Spain initially tried to emulate Portuguese trafficking by despatching ships from Seville to West Africa with the express purpose of procuring Africans. Prevented from continuing this practice by the Treaty of Tordesillas, Spain introduced a licensing system in 1518 to meet the demand for African labour in its New World mines. Holders of licences were obliged to secure their captured Africans from the Portuguese and register their ships at Seville. Though this system largely failed because of abuse and inability of licencees to supply the requisite number of Africans, it lasted until the end of the sixteenth century. During the period of unification with Portugal, a new system was adopted called the asiento in 1595. This aimed to regularise and regulate the trafficking as well as generate more revenue for the Crown. The asiento was effectively a monopoly contract that was given to a foreign company or country in return for a fixed fee or percentage. Increasingly the asiento became an instrument of European power politics and passed from hand to hand depending on the prevailing political climate: from Portugal to Genoa, to the Netherlands, to France, and to the United Kingdom in 1713. In 1750 the United Kingdom gave up the asiento, and the decision was taken to give it to Spanish merchants.

From the 1770s onwards, with the Treaty of Tordesillas torn to shreds by the entry of other European countries into the trafficking of Africans and their grabbing of bits of the Spanish empire, a free trade policy was promulgated as a means of quickly resolving the desperate shortage of labour in Cuba caused by an epidemic which had killed 17,000 enslaved Africans.

Spanish involvement in the trafficking of Africans was given a significant boost when the Haitian Revolution effectively destroyed Saint Domingue as the major sugar producer in the world and led to an inflation in sugar prices in Europe. Within two decades, Cuba had become the third largest sugar producer in the world. Whereas in earlier decades the distribution of Africans had been to territories such as Mexico, Colombia, Panama, Ecuador, Venezuela, Uruguay, Paraguay, Peru, Dominican Republic and even Argentina and Chile, the movement of Africans now favoured Cuba and Puerto Rico.

In 1820 a treaty was signed outlawing the trafficking In Africans. Spain, however, simply adopted a strategy of trafficking under Portuguese and American flags. A further treaty was signed in 1862 to outlaw the trafficking. The last recorded Spanish slaving ship arrived in Cuba in 1867. Though slavery was outlawed in many Spanish territories in the struggle for national independence, it continued in the Spanish colonies like Cuba until 1886.

While Spanish trafficking never amounted to more than 10 percent of volume of Africans transported, Spanish demand fuelled the trafficking undertaken by other European countries.

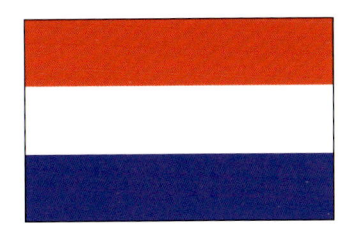

NETHERLANDS

On the eve of the seventeenth century, the Netherlands had broken away from its Spanish overlords and began to engage in an aggressive campaign of colonial expansion. Though a small country lacking in natural resources, the Netherlands was able to become the centre for European overseas trade, including the trafficking in Africans, during the seventeenth century. The first recorded transport of Africans by the Dutch was the group of 20 who were sold to the colony of Virginia in North America in 1619. The formation of the Dutch West India Company in 1621 was to transform the country's involvement.

Conceived as a weapon of economic warfare against Spain, the company was given a charter to ship, trade, build fortresses, and maintain troops, garrisons and fleets. With their large, heavily armed ships, they began to harass and attack Spanish/Portuguese shipping and trading posts in Africa and Asia with considerable success. Wars with Portugal (1620-1655) left the Dutch in control of many of the slave factories on the West African coast, centred on modern Ghana such as São Jorge da Mina (renamed Elmina), which they captured from the Portuguese in 1637. By 1650 the Dutch had already dispatched 30,000 Africans to Brazil alone.

The Dutch conquered and briefly held some Portuguese plantation colonies in Brazil. They also had control over territory in Eastern United States as well as the Caribbean islands of Curacao (a great slaving depot), Aruba, Tobago and a few smaller ones. Access to the conquered north Brazilian (New Holland) market is what led to the take off of Dutch trafficking in Africans after many Portuguese planters decided to remain under Dutch overlordship. Even after a combined Spanish-Portuguese force had recovered most of the conquered territories in 1654, Dutch traders were able to draw upon their network of forts to supply other European powers, dominating the supply to Spain until the 1690s. Dutch innovation in shipbuilding led to the development of efficient designs such as the 'Fluyt' or 'fly boat', whose pre-fabricated parts, vast cargo hold, and shallow draft gave it a decided advantage in African coastal waters. By the end of the seventeenth century they had a fleet of such vessels trading on the West African coast all year round from a number of ports in the Netherlands: Amsterdam, Rotterdam and the Zeeland ports of Flushing, Vlissingen and Middleburg. The development of these ports gave rise to independent slaving companies, the largest being the Middleburg Commercial Company, which was responsible for transporting over 30,000 Africans to the Americas.

For a short moment, the Dutch became the world's major slaving nation. They even provided the investment capital that underwrote the trafficking ventures of other nations such as Denmark, Sweden, Latvia and Brandenburg (Prussia). The centre of Dutch trafficking in Africans between 1670 and 1815 was the Caribbean island of Curaçao which became their main entrepôt for supplying South American and Caribbean plantations with Africans held at two camps on the island – Sorsaka and Chinco Grandi (present day Groot St Joris) – pending sale.

Castle Cormantine, Ghana (later Fort Amsterdam). Located in the Fante kingdom of Efutu, Africans deported from here were known collectively in Caribbean as Coromantees, though coming from different African groups such as the Ashanti. Mid seventeenth century copperplate engraving (detail) by John Ogilby, in O. Dapper (1670/1976) *Beschreibung von Afrika*.

What the Dutch had achieved other nations such as Britain and France strove to replicate. Constant wars with Spain, France and Britain eventually sapped Dutch power, and their involvement in the trade began to decline at the end of the seventeenth century. Most devastating for the Dutch was the passing of the Navigation Acts which forbade the importation of captured Africans into English and French colonies except in French and English ships. This effectively deprived the Dutch of the 'middleman role' which had underpinned their success. Though having bases in Ghana, the Dutch lacked significant markets comparable to Portuguese Brazil, French Saint Domingue, or British Jamaica. The Dutch West India Company effectively ceased trading in 1795. It is estimated that the company had transported over 550,000 Africans. The abolition of Dutch trafficking in Africans had no impact on slavery in the Dutch territories. Slavery continued until it was abolished in 1863.

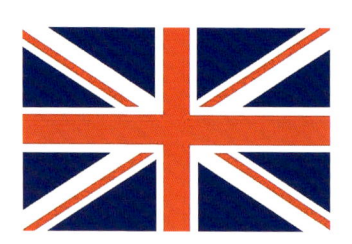

UNITED KINGDOM

The British may not have initiated the trafficking in Africans, nor did they did cling to it the longest, but they, more than any other nation, perfected the system and raised it to new heights of refined complexity and profitability.

Official British involvement in the trafficking in Africans, lasting some 245 years, started when Sir John Hawkins captured 300 Africans in 1562 and sold them illegally to the Spanish. There is evidence, however, that British merchants had, for decades before that, bought and sold Africans in Andalucia (Spain). It is also known too that, because of the alliance that Elizabeth I had cultivated with the ruler of Morocco, Mulay Ahmad al-Mansur, against their mutual enemy, Spain, English merchants, most notably the Barbary Company formed in 1585, had strategically sold munitions to the Moroccan army and navy. Such weapons enabled Al-Mansur to defeat the Songhay Empire in 1591 and secure control of its gold trade as a source of finance for imperial expansion. The resultant destruction and fragmentation of this important centre of political stability in West Africa was to have lasting repercussions on the ability of Europeans to extend their influence in West Africa.

British involvement in the slave trade was given impetus by the acquisition of territories in the Caribbean and North America during the course of the seventeenth century. Colonies were established in St Kitts (1624), Barbados (1627), Nevis (1628), Antigua and Montserrat (1632), Jamaica (1655), Cayman Is (1655), Virgin Islands (1666), and Bahamas (1670). The need to provide labour to these colonies, particularly to Jamaica, led to the setting up of a number of royal companies.

In 1663 King Charles II set up the first dedicated slaving company, the Company of Royal Adventurers Trading to Africa, with a monopoly charter. This replaced the earlier private Guinea Company of Adventurers of London Trading to the Ports of Africa set up in 1618 by Robert Rich, the Virginia tobacco planter who later became the Earl of Warwick. The Company of Royal Adventurers collapsed in 1667 after the war with the Dutch and was replaced in 1672 by the Royal African Company. For the next 20 years this London-based, royal monopoly (with the Duke of York – later James II – as a major shareholder) was charged with developing and maintaining

Cabo Corso (short cape) was originally built as a small trading lodge by the Portuguese. It passed into the hands of the British in 1664 and was re-named Cape Coast Castle. Holding up to 1,500 Africans at any one time, the castle served as the seat of British administration in Ghana until victory in the Ashanti wars enabled the British government to move to the more central location of Accra (Christianborg Castle) in 1877.
Photo: Yamagata Hiroo. Source: www.flickr.com

a number of forts along the African coast in order to prosecute the trafficking in Africans, and contest vigorously Dutch hegemony of the trade. The Company was responsible for importing over 150,000 Africans into the Caribbean.

The end of another European war in 1698 and the resultant destruction of the main British slaving fort of Fort James (Gambia) found the company in grave financial trouble. Unwilling to foot the bill for rebuilding the fort, Parliament acceded to the lobby by private merchants from Bristol for the dismantling of the company's monopoly. On payment of a duty of 10 percent – rescinded in 1712 – private merchants could now enter the traffic. With the ending of the War of Spanish Succession and the signing of the Treat of Utrecht in 1713, the recently unified United Kingdom gained control over the Spanish asiento, a contract to supply the Spanish colonies with 144,000 Africans a year. With these transformations, the centre of gravity shifted from London to Bristol and thence to Liverpool. The opening up of the trafficking and the shift in gravity to Bristol propelled towns like Birmingham to prominence as suppliers of important trade good such guns, fetters, shackles, chains – what became known in the business as Brummagem ware, because of their supposedly cheap quality. The firm of Farmer & Galton (later Galton & Son) – both coming from Quaker families – came to symbolise the role played by the town in arming the slave trade, in other words, providing the weapons that would fuel internecine conflict in West Africa. It is estimate that Europe exported over 20,000,000 guns to Africa during the eighteenth century.

The risky and long-term nature of the trafficking gave rise to important banking houses that could offer credit to traders. Such was the service provided by Alexander and David Barclay that led eventually to the Barclays Bank. The Bank of England also featured heavily in the trafficking.

Bance Island, ca.1805. One of the main trading forts/factories established by the British (Royal African Company) in 1672 for processing African captives. The factory included a 'great house' for the Chief Agent, quarters for captives, officials and soldiers, a jetty and a fortification with 16 cannons. Joseph Corry, *Observations upon the Widward Coast*, British Library Board. All rights reserved 072808.

At the height of the trafficking co-ordinated by the new Company of Merchants, British traders transported more Africans than any other maritime nation: 3.1 million between 1662 and 1807. Between 1698 and 1807, 11,000 ships sailed from British ports such as London, Bristol, Liverpool, Lancaster and Whitehaven. Amongst the many slave traders there were many who were Quakers. The trade was seen as 'in perfect harmony with the principles of the Word of God.'

The rising tide of rebellions amongst enslaved Africans and the growing abolitionist campaigns led to the abolition of the British slave trade in 1807. Having trafficked in Africans for 245 years, the British now sought to claim the high moral ground by converting the Royal Navy from protector of slaving ships to self-proclaimed policemen of the high seas with a duty to confiscate the cargoes of foreign ships. The sense of moral righteousness that underpinned the anti-slaving patrols set up by the British off the coast of Africa and Brazil unquestionably rested on the country's unchallenged naval power.

The irony is that there was a significant British interest in the continued trafficking. No sooner had the 1807 Slave Trade Abolition Act been passed, that British slave traders and financiers adopted ways for circumventing the legislation: fitting out ships en route, flying under different flags, and most, significant of all, financially sponsoring the slave trade of other countries. Given the increasing pre-eminence of British manufacturing, it is not surprising to find that British-made goods tended to find their way into the trafficking in Africans

The Abolition of the Slave Trade did not lead to the ending of slavery. This took another 31 years.

FRANCE

French involvement in the trafficking of Africans goes back to the 1540s when small traders sought illegally to supply the Spanish colonies. The real impetus for French involvement came in the 1620s onwards, after France had acquired a number of Caribbean possessions: St Kitts (1625), Martinique (1635), Guadeloupe (1635), Dominica (1635), Cayenne (1635), Grenada (1650) and St Domingue – Haiti (1660), and Louisiana (1699).

As in the British territories, the French initially experimented with white indentured workers or engagés but these were rapidly superseded by the use of Africans. Following a series of failed initiatives, the French government, in 1635, established a West Indian company to provide Africans for its developing Caribbean plantations. In 1664, this was replaced by a new government-financed monopoly company, Compagnie des Indes Occidentales. To ensure the success of this company, the government offered a bounty of ten livres for every African transported to the Caribbean. The success of this bounty led to the formation, in 1673, of a private company, Compagnie du Sénégal, which took as its main aim the trafficking in Africans.

A necessary component of this reorganisation of French trafficking in Africans was the acquisition of African bases. The initial base developed at St Louis in 1638 was extended to incorporate Gorée (1677), and Assimie (1687) in the basin of River Senegal. A foothold was also established at Whydah in Dahomey. It is from these areas

'La vente des Nègrés' (French slave market), Musée des Ducs de Bretagne, Nantes, 1848.

that France was to derive the majority of its enslaved Africans.

In 1701, with the rapprochement between Spain and France that resulted from the accession of the Bourbon Philip V to the Spanish throne, the French Guinea Company was granted a 10-year contract, the asiento, to supply Spanish America with Africans. Defeat in the War of Spanish Succession meant that the lucrative asiento passed to the British. This loss was more than compensated by the increasing demand for Africans in the French Caribbean territories. Indeed, in order to meet this demand, the French continued to rely on other nations for a third of its needs. To stimulate further French involvement, measures were introduced in 1716 and 1717 to open out the trafficking to private traders. The bounty offered by the government was increased to 100 livres, and again to 160 in 1787. By the 1760s the number of slaving ships leaving French ports every year stood at 56. While seemingly small, i.e. in comparison to the number leaving British ports, French ships were generally larger, with an average capacity of 364 Africans.

Throughout the eighteenth century, French involvement in the trafficking of Africans grew rapidly making them the third largest trafficker (behind Britain and Portugal) by the end of the century. In the first eight decades of the eighteenth century over 1.25 million Africans were transported across the Atlantic by over 3,000 French ships sailing from the main slaving ports of Nantes, Bordeaux, La Rochelle, Le Havre, and St Malo. St Domingue (Haiti) was the most significant destination for these ships. From a population of 2,000 Africans in the 1680s, the African population in Saint Domingue rose to 460,000 in the 1780s. The island had become the largest sugar producer in the French Empire, sucking in half of all the Africans imported into the Caribbean by the French.

The outbreak of the French Revolution in 1789, followed soon after by the start of the Haitian Revolution in 1791, disrupted French involvement in the trafficking in Africans. Consequent on events taking place in St Domingue, the National Convention in 1794 passed a decree to abolish slavery and the slave trade in the French territories. On coming to power, Napoleon rescinded this decree in 1802, and despatched troops to the colonies to reinstitute slavery and the slave trade. While the French managed to successfully put down resistance and reintroduce slavery into the Caribbean territories of Martinique and Guadeloupe, their attempts to do likewise in Saint Domingue, by despatching a 30,000 Expeditionary Force to the island under the command of General Leclerc, was defeated by Dessalines. Haiti declared its independence on January 1st, 1804.

After the restoration of the Bourbon monarchy in 1815, France formally abolished the slave trade in 1818. National honour, however, ensured that they would not tolerate the British Navy boarding and searching French ships. Invoking national pride, French merchants from Nantes and Bordeaux continued to traffic in Africans illicitly until 1830 when Louis-Phillippe passed a new law to make trafficking a crime enforceable by punishment. Under this law, the French acquiesced to the searching of French ships by the British Navy in certain cases. As late as 1848 Africans were still being imported into Martinique and Guadeloupe. Spurred on by uprisings amongst enslaved Africans, slavery was abolished in the French territories in 1848. A year later plantation owners were awarded 120 million francs in compensation.

'Vue du Cap Français et du navire, *La Marie Seraphique*', Musée des Ducs de Bretagne. Third voyage of French slave ship, *La Marie Seraphique* from Nantes, 1772, off the coast of Haiti with Angolan captives for sale.

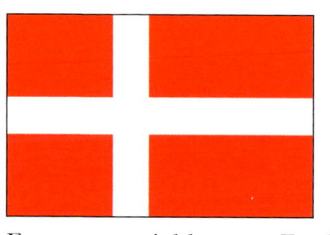

DENMARK-NORWAY

Denmark-Norway – then a unified kingdom – was the last European country to participate in the European trafficking in Africans. Their buying, transporting and selling of captured Africans lasted 196 years. In the wake of a costly war with Sweden, Denmark-Norway sought quickly to recover its economic fortune by adopting the trafficking route to economic aggrandisement followed by its larger European neighbours – England, France, Spain and Portugal. By the 1640s the Danes were despatching slaving ships to Guinea. Their involvement became more organised when they chartered the Gluckstadt company to expand the trade. The *Neldebladet*, owned by the Secretary of the Exchequer in Copenhagen, Jens Lassen, was the first Danish ship to supply Africans to the Caribbean in 1651.

The possession of ships was never a sufficient basis for gaining a foothold in the trafficking in Africans. An important second step was the acquisition of trading/military forts along the African coast where organised trafficking could be conducted with local merchants and African leaders. In 1657, the Danes acquired several Swedish forts in Ghana. To exert influence in the Volta region and the 'Slave Coast' of Togo and Benin and thereby secure a competitive edge, they proceeded to build a number of forts/trading lodges under the patronage and protection of local African leaders: Fort Fredriksborg (1660), Fort Christiansborg at Osu (1661), Fort Fredensborg at Old Ningo (1736-42), Fort Kongensten at Ada (1783), Fort Prinsensten at Keta (1784), Fort Augustaborg at Teshie (1787), and Fort Isegram (Isegraae) at Kpone (1787). Through such forts Denmark/Norway could meet its own demands and supply the Portuguese who had been long squeezed out from the Gold Coast region.

Overseeing Danish involvement in the trafficking in Africans was the Danish West India & Guinea Company which was given a royal charter in 1671 to trade in Africans and manage Danish business in Africa and the Caribbean. Through arrangements with other European countries, particularly the French and the Spanish, whose supply always fell short of demand, the West India and Guinea Company gained access to lucrative Caribbean markets. Recognising the need for guaranteed market outlets in a volatile Caribbean region dominated by bigger players, the Danes quickly acquired or purchased a number of islands – St Thomas, St John, and St Croix – where sugar plantations could be developed. In 1754 the Danish West India and Guinea Company was bought by the Kingdom of Denmark-Norway. One of the best documented Danish slave ships is the *Fredensborg* which was built in Copenhagen in 1753. On the third leg of the Triangular Trade – the Caribbean to Europe – in 1768, the *Fredensborg* sank in a storm close to the island of Tromøy in sourthern Norway.

Danish slave ship, the *Fredensborg*, loading Africans at Christiansborg Castle in Ghana, April 1768. Drawing by Chr Bøgø, 1927. Courtesy of Leif Svalesen.

In 1792, the unified kingdom became the first European country to abolish the trafficking in Africans. The 1792 Abolition Act however allowed traders a ten year grace before the measure came into force in 1803. The last decade was a period of aggressive trafficking by the Danes with 30,000 Africans shipped to the Caribbean. Illicit trafficking continued until the 1830s and 1840s at Danish forts. Trafficking in ships flying the Danish flag between 1660 and 1806 accounted for the movement of 85,000 Africans. This figure excludes the 70,000 Africans purchased from other carriers and re-exported to other islands.

As in the case of other European countries, the abolition of trafficking did not lead to the abolition of slavery. Slavery continued in the Danish West Indies until 1848 when enslaved Africans staged a non-violent, mass demonstration that forced Governor General von Scholten to declare general emancipation throughout the Danish islands. Soon after, in 1850, Denmark-Norway gave up its colonial ambitions and disposed of its African forts and factories in Ghana to Britain.

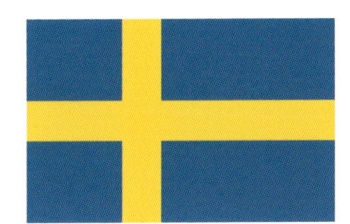

SWEDEN

In the middle of the seventeenth century King Gustavus Adolphus of Sweden entered into negotiations with the Dutch West India Company in order to secure a foothold in the trafficking in Africans. A Swedish African Company, financed in Amsterdam, was formed in 1647 for this purpose, and a number of joint ventures between the Swedes and the Dutch took place with the former supplying the ships and crews for the voyages, while the latter supplied the captains and the finance. In 1652, Sweden took over Cape Coast from the Dutch and built Carolusburg Castle (now known as Cape Coast Castle) in 1653. When Sweden's North American colony of New Sweden (Delaware) was taken over by the Dutch in 1655, an important rationale for Swedish involvement in the trafficking of Africans disappeared. After the war with Denmark, the four Swedish forts in Ghana were seized by the Danes in 1657, bringing to an end the first period of Swedish involvement in the trafficking of Africans.

The desire of Gustav III to re-establish Sweden as a European power laid the basis for a second Swedish attempt to get involved in the trafficking in Africans. In 1784, Sweden bought the Caribbean island of Saint-Barthélemy from the French. Two years later, a Swedish West India Company was established with the king as the largest stockholder. The company was given a charter to traffick in captured Africans. With Saint-Barthorélemy unsuitable for sugar cultivation – much of it being sterile rock and poor soil – the company sought to turn the island into a free trade area from which other European countries could buy Africans at competitive prices, i.e. without the taxes that were often imposed in the different Caribbean territories. The company hoped that they could supply the French market, particularly in Saint Domingue (Haiti). The outbreak of the Haitian Revolution scuppered this ambition. The Swedish slaving project limped along until the government, struggling financially, decided to abandon the idea of using trafficking as a route to European power. Exactly how many Africans were brought to the Americas in Swedish ships is impossible to say. It is estimated to be not more than 2,000.

Africans being rowed out to waiting Danish slave ship, the *Fredensborg*, 1768. Courtesy of Ants Lepson.

DUCHY OF COURLAND (LATVIA)

It was not only large countries that sought to develop colonies and benefit from the trafficking in Africans. The Duchy of Courland (Latvia), then a vassal state of the Polish-Lithuanian Commonwealth, represents a forgotten chapter in the history of the Caribbean and the slave trade. Possessing one of the largest merchant fleets in Europe at the time, the Duchy's leader, Duke Jacob Kettler, built Jekabsforts (Fort James) on St Andrews island (James Island) in the River Gambia in 1651. With a toehold gained in Africa, Duke Jacob redoubled the efforts that had been made since 1637 to establish successful settlements in the Caribbean. After a fourth attempt, a new colony, also called Jekabsfort, was founded in Tobago or New Courland as it was then called. The most significant support for the Courland venture came from England which, under Cromwell, signed a treaty of neutrality in 1654. The invasion of the Duchy by the Swedes in the late 1650s provided an opportunity for the Dutch to seize the Courland Tobago settlements, and to destroy the merchant fleet and factories. Though Tobago was returned to the Duchy after the Treaty of Oliwa (1660), the inability to restore the fleet to its pre-war glory led to the abandonment of Tobago in 1690, when the island was sold.

BRANDENBURG-PRUSSIA

With the assistance of a Dutch merchant, Benjamin Raule, Friedrich Wilhelm, Elector of Brandenburg, sought to emulate the 'Africa policy' of his uncle Jacob, Duke of Courland. The Elector hoped that the acquisition of a fleet of ships able to participate in the trafficking in Africans would help Brandenburg to overcome the devastation caused by the Thirty Years' War (1618-48). In 1682, the Amsterdam-financed Brandenburg African Company, with its headquarters in Emden, was established to co-ordinate Brandenburg involvement. A year later, a major fortress complex known as Gross Friedrichsburg was built in Ghana under Fante overlordship. Smaller outposts were established at Accada, Taccrama and Taccorary. Thus began Prussian attempts to compete in the international trading networks that had enriched other European nations.

The company operated out of Gross Friedrichsburg for nearly forty years achieving its high point in 1686. Possessing no Caribbean plantation that could function as an outlet for the Africans taken across the Atlantic, the Brandenburg African Company sought quickly to sign a treaty with the Danish West India Company which gave it a trading post on the Danish Caribbean island of St Thomas (Virgin Islands). Though this gave it access to Caribbean markets, the company had to pay duties to the Danes who determined the price for Africans. Plagued by mis-management, constant competition from European rivals and piracy, the company failed to make the impact that the Elector had hoped. By the time Friedrich III had ascended to the Prussian throne, interest in the enterprise had waned, and the property in Ghana was sold to the Dutch in 1717. It is estimated that the Brandenburg Company was responsible for shipping between 10,000 and 30,000 Africans to the Americas.

It was a further 150 years before Germany sought to acquire another foothold on the African continent.

Gold coins produced by the Elector of Brandenburg to symbolise the Brandenburg presence in the slave trade. The gold was quite likely obtained in Ghana.

Forts/Factories: Legacies in Stone

Up and down the coast of West Africa one finds the remnants of a string of forts/castles/factories that today represent a mute testimony – a legacy in stone – to an unparalleled coming and going of humanity – and inhumanity. From the moment that the Portuguese established a fort on the island of Arguin in 1445 to facilitate their search for gold and enslaved Africans, other European nations followed suit and, over the next four centuries, built similar forts/factories to enable them to get a share of the West African trade. Nowhere in Africa is the density of forts greater than in modern-day Ghana.

The location chosen for the forts was generally the mouth of a river with easy access to the interior of the continent. Sometimes offshore islands or rocky promontories were selected as sites for forts for health and security reasons, e.g. Gorée. Construction generally took place under the overlordship of a local ruler to whom ground rent would be paid. Forts were generally under the command of a governor or commandant. The complement of fort staff also included detachments of soldiers, clerks, mechanics, priests, castle slave servants, and junior factors whose job it was to exchange European manufactured goods for Africans, gold dust and ivory. The forts were in effect mini city-states. They were commercial centres and military establishments. Lager forts sometimes had up to 50-60 mounted cannons to repel any attempted siege by a European force or by a local African group. Yet this did not prevent changing ownership. A typical example here would be Cape Coast Castle.

Forts were the factories that processed the goods obtained locally for shipment to Europe or to the Caribbean. Over time the processing of Africans became the major activity of most factories. In the dark, damp and cramped conditions of the male and female dungeons, a fort like Elmina could easily imprison 1,500 Africans at any one time pending the arrival of a slave ship, which sometimes took months. Forts were built with maximum security in mind. Dungeons tended to have extremely small apertures that allowed only for the circulation of air and the extrusion of urine. The only way out of a fort for captives was the 'Door of No Return' through which millions of Africans were deported to begin the Middle Passage journey to the Americas. By the end of the eighteenth century, 30,000 Africans passed through Elmina each year. Captured Africans held in fort dungeons would have come from different cultural/ethnic groups and spoke several languages. Being God-fearing people, European fort officials built their churches over, or next to, the dungeons where captured Africans were inhumanely kept. Inside the Dutch chapel on the second floor at Elmina there is an inscription in Dutch from Psalm 132:14: "This is my resting place forever and ever; here I will sit enthroned, for I have desired it." Translating the inscription the guide stated: "Apparently, God lived in this room alone; they didn't let him out." A trapdoor in the Governor's quarters ensured that any female captive who caught the Governor's eye could be brought upstairs to do the Governor's bidding.

In the fifteenth century, Europeans understood quickly that trade with African kingdoms, and especially the trafficking in Africans, would only be possible by building a cordon which effectively hemmed in their African partners and circumscribed their ability to play one European country off against another. In return for support, local traders and leaders were offered protection and refuge when the area came under attack. The actual power

Above: Plan der Festung Großfriedrichsburg (Plan of Fort Grossfriedrichsburg), built by the Elector of Brandenburg in 1683 to prosecute the slave trade in Ghana. Source: Deutsches Historisches Museum, Berlin.
Below: 'House of Slaves' staircase leading to the 'Door of No Return', Gorée Island. Photo: bdinphoenix. Source: Flickr.com

MAIN GHANAIAN FORTS

Accra - Fort Crevecoer (Ussher Fort)
Accra - Christianborg Castle
Accra - Fort James
Ada - Fort Kongesten
Ankobra - Fort Eliza Cathargo
Anomabu - Fort William
Apam - Fort Leydsaemheyt (Fort Patience)
Axim - Fort San Antonio
Beyin - Fort Appolonia
Butri - Fort Batensteyn
Cape Coast - Cape Coast Castle
Cape Coast - Fort McCarthy
Cape Coast - Morie Fort Nassau
Cape Coast - Fort Victoria
Cape Coast - Fort William
Dixcove - Fort Metal Cross
Elmina - Fort St. Jago (Conraadsburg)
Elmina - Fort St. Jorge (Elmina Castle)
Keta - Fort Prinsenstein
Komenda - Fort Vredenburg
Kormantse - Fort Amsterdam
Kwida - Fort Dorothea
Prampram - Fort Yernon
Princesstown - Gross-Friedrichsburg or Fort Hollandia
Sekondi - Fort Orange
Senya Beraku - Fort Goedehoop (Good Hope)
Shama - Fort St. Sebastian
Takrama - Fort Sophie Louise
Teshie - Fort Augustaborg

Right: 'Door of No Return', Gorée Island, Senegal. Photo: Galen R. Frysinger.
Far right: Dungeon with air vent. La Maison des Esclaves (Slave House), Gorée Island, Senegal. Photo: Galen R. Frysinger.

of the fort, however, did not generally extend beyond the range of the cannons. By constituting a zone of influence, too, European rivals would thereby be encouraged to utilise the trading facilities of the forts to acquire captive Africans, unless they too had their own forts, local alliances and spheres of influence. It was with a view to developing such alliances and to building up their strength locally, that the Dutch set about building Fort Nassau near Cape Coast Castle from which they were able to successfully attack the Portuguese stronghold of Elmina and oust them in 1637. Victory at Elmina was to usher in a 235 year period of Dutch occupation of the fort.

A change in European tenure of a local fort sometimes offered opportunities for local African groups to seize control of the fort themselves. Such was the situation in 1717 when the Brandenburg African Company vacated Fort Gross-Friedrichsburg in favour of the Dutch. A Chief of the Ahanta people, John Conny, the 'Black Prussian', captured the fort and, for a time, successfully repelled Dutch attempts to occupy the fort. His heroic efforts are still immortalised in the John Conny (Canoe) festival in islands like Jamaica, where many of the Ahanta people ended up after their resistance was finally crushed.

In the nineteenth century these forts were to provide a springboard from which Europeans could launch their full-scale takeover of the continent.

EUROPEAN INVOLVEMENT IN THE SLAVE TRADE

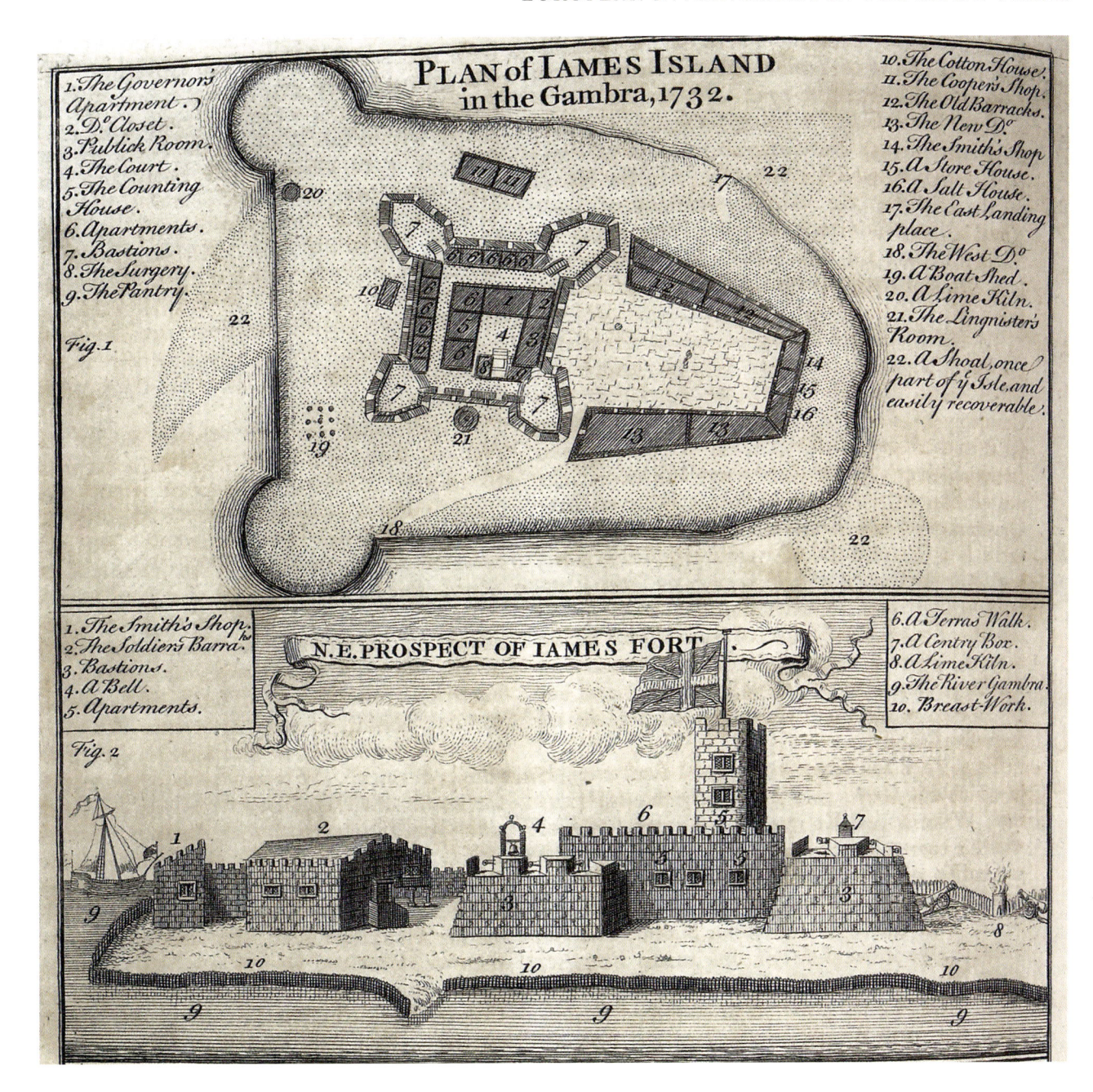

'…such is the Nature of that Country that all Nations have judged it impracticable to support their claim to it without Forts, the more effectually to encourage the Natives to bring their Trade and to give weight to their alliances with them, as these are facts incontestable, sure no person that has the least Knowledge of that Country will say the Trade to Africa can be preserved to Great Britain, without Forts being properly maintained and supported, upon those parts where other European powers have them'.

Earl of Dartmouth, *A Proposal for Putting the Forts on the Coast of Africa under the Direction of the Lords of Trade and Plantation*, 1765. Staffordshire Record Office.

James Island Fort, Gambia. Originally built by the Duchy of Courland (Latvia) in 1651, the fort was taken over by the English in 1661, when it became Britain's first imperial posession in Africa. Illustration: John Green (?), *A New General Collection of Voyages & Travels*. British Library Board. All rights reserved 082075.

3

The Middle Passage

Dr Clive Harris

African captives were allocated a space six feet long and sixteen inches wide.

'The second mate and boatswain descend into the hold, whip in hand, and range the slaves in their regular places; those on the right side of the vessel facing forward, lying in each other's lap, while those on the left are similarly stowed with their faces towards the stern. In this way each negro lies on his right side, which is considered preferable for the action of the heart. In allotting places, particular attention is paid to size, the taller being selected for the greatest breadth of the vessel, while the shorter and younger are lodged near the bows.'

Capt. Theodore Canot,
Twenty Years of an African Slave Trader, 1854.

By the Middle Passage we are talking about that second leg of the Triangular Trade, the hellish oceanic journey of European slave ships across the Atlantic Ocean that forcibly estranged and separated millions of Africans from their homes and communities in Africa and scattered them throughout the length and breadth of the Americas, from Canada down to Argentina, and throughout the archipelago of Caribbean islands. Scholars have made their careers disputing whether it was ten, twelve, fifteen, twenty or more million Africans who were transported to the Americas by the 30,000 and more documented journeys made by European slave ships across the Atlantic Ocean. Important though it is to have an accurate actuarial history, this exercise should never deflect us away from making sense of the magnitude of the crime against humanity inflicted on Africans from first to last moment of the Middle Passage. Millions more set out but did not arrive in the Americas. Their bones litter the well-furrowed pathway that is understood as the Middle Passage.

DEPORTATION FROM AFRICA

Having been marched for months from the interior to the coast, or ferried down river in canoes and then confined in factories/forts and barracoons on the coast pending the arrival of a slave ship, African captives were now to embark on a journey for which they had no cultural frame of comprehension, and across an ocean that most had never seen. If rumour was to be believed, they were being taken by Europeans to be eaten, to be made into oil or gunpowder, or to be used to dye the flags of Spanish ships red.

It took traders weeks, sometimes months, to assemble a sufficient cargo of Africans depending on the area of the African coast where ships were anchored and the number of ships from other nations also in the vicinity. Africans selected for purchase were minutely and intrusively inspected from head to toe for the slightest sign of any physical affliction with complete disregard to personal dignity. In the European mind it was inconceivable that the captives could resist this normalising judgment about the fitness of the African's anatomy for plantation labour. Before embarkation, the heads of captives were shaved and, in instances where the cargo belonged to different owners, the brand of each was impressed onto the African's body. On being brought aboard, Africans were stripped of all clothing, and sent into the hold of the ship naked, ostensibly as 'the only means of securing cleanliness and health'. Iron restraints called bilboes (leg irons) and handcuffs were imposed on all men, two by two, i.e. right leg to left leg, right hand to left hand. The next step in governing the African, was to allocate them to their appropriate space in the hold of the ship.

On a typical slave ship, each man was allocated a space six feet long and sixteen inches wide (and usually about two feet seven inches high). Every woman was allocated a space five feet ten inches long by sixteen inches wide. Every boy was allocated a space of five feet by fourteen inches; every girl, four feet six inches by twelve inches.

European slave traders debated at length the relative merits of 'loose packing' and 'tight packing'. 'Loose packers' believed that by giving Africans more space and better food, mortality rates would be lower and prices in Caribbean markets higher. 'Tight packers' argued that while the loss of life might be greater, it was compensated for by the higher receipts for the larger cargo of Africans. In any case, survivors could easily be fattened up before being offered for sale. 'Tight packing' won out. Slavers crammed every nook and cranny, sometimes well above the legal limit, and trusted to fair winds and maximum speed across the Atlantic to minimise casualties.

Once captives had been securely stowed, guards were placed on the hatchways. At their ready disposition was a range of small arms, loaded and primed for action, together with some Granada shells. As was customary on slave ships, swivel blunderbusses supplied by companies such as Farmer & Galton in Birmingham (UK) were trained on the holds to counteract any insurrection.

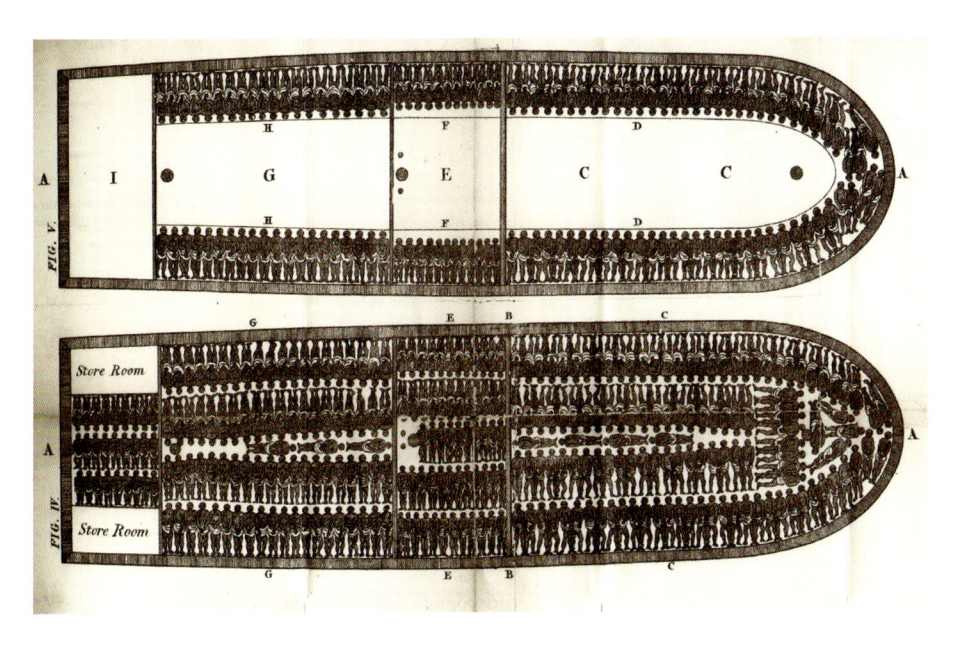

Diagram of Liverpool slave ship *The Brookes*, carrying 454 Africans. In earlier voyages, it had carried 609-740 Africans. Courtesy of Birmingham Archives & Heritage.

African captives whipped and forced to dance to prevent 'melancholic death'. *La France Maritime* by Amédée Gréhan (ed.), Paris 1837.

MIDDLE PASSAGE AS A CROSSROADS OF DISEASE

The time taken by a ship to cross the Atlantic depended upon a variety of factors: point of origin in Africa, destination in the Americas, and conditions at sea such as winds, currents, and storms. With favourable winds over the shortest journey – say, Gambia to Barbados or Angola to Brazil – the journey might take three to four weeks. When ships were becalmed in the doldrums, or encountered storms, the journey could take more than three months.

Whatever the length of the journey, overcrowding and the associated problems of cleanliness, sanitation and hygiene were virtually insuperable, and disease claimed many victims. The middle passage was in effect a crossroads and market place for disease. European diseases such small pox, measles, gonorrhoea, and syphilis combined with African diseases such as yellow and dengue fever, amoebic and bacillary dysentery. Epidemics raged aboard many slave ships carrying away many. The most common and devastating epidemic was dysentery, generally referred to as the (white) flux. Next in severity were small pox and measles. Ships were not equipped to

> 'But whenever the sea is rough, and the rain heavy, it becomes necessary to shut the [air vents], …the negroes rooms very soon grow intolerably hot. The confined air, rendered noxious by the effluvia exhaled from their bodies, and by being repeatedly breathed, soon produces fevers and fluxes, which generally carries off great numbers of them…
>
> '…But the excessive heat was not the only thing that rendered the situation intolerable. The deck, that is, the floor of their rooms, was so covered with the blood and mucus which had proceeded from them in consequence of the flux, that it resembled a slaughter-house. It is not in the power of the human imagination, to picture to itself a situation more dreadful or disgusting. Numbers of the slaves having fainted, they were carried on deck, where several of them died, and the rest were, with great difficulty, restored…
>
> 'The surgeon, upon going between decks, in the morning, to examine the situation of the slaves, frequently found several dead; and among the men, sometimes a dead and living negro fastened by their irons together. When this is the case, they are brought upon the deck, and laid on the grating, the living negro is disengaged, and the dead one thrown overboard.'
>
> 'Exercise deemed necessary for the preservation of their health, they are sometimes obliged to dance, when the weather will permit their coming on deck. If they go about it reluctantly, or do not move with agility, they are flogged, a person standing by them all the time with a cat-o'-nine-tails in his hand for that purpose… The poor wretches are frequently compelled to sing also; but when they do, their songs are generally, as may naturally be expected, melancholy lamentations of their exile from their native country.'
>
> Alexander Falconbridge, *An Account of the Slave Trade On the Coast of Africa*, 1788.

deal with epidemics. Most ships carried medicine and a couple of surgeons but their skill did not often extend beyond separating the sick from the apparently healthy to protect the valuable investment. Those suspected of harbouring a contagious infection would be unceremoniously tossed overboard. In extreme circumstances, half the Africans might die. Even after the passing of the Dolben Act (1788) designed to regularise conditions aboard slave ships, the average mortality rate was still high in 1789, 12.5 percent. Deaths on slave ships were so frequent that the crewmen often told of schools of sharks that followed ships all the way across the Atlantic Ocean. Mortality rates were higher for men than for women.

Another condition that was said to be responsible for many deaths amongst Africans was what surgeons diagnosed as 'fixed melancholia'. Falconbridge believed this condition to be one of the greatest causes of mortality. An African captive suffering from this condition seemed to go into a deep depression and will himself/herself to death. Some African groups such as Igbos were described as being more prone to this act of willed death. Africans were constantly monitored to identify the early signs of 'fixed melancholia'.

Willed death was only one form of suicide common amongst captives. Many attempted to commit suicide by throwing themselves overboard. This practice was also said to be more prevalent amongst Igbos who believed that 'when they die they return home to their own country and friends again.' In fitting out ships, this soon led to the practice of rigging nets to prevent people throwing themselves overboard.

For those who persisted in the belief that suicide offered a form of salvation, the captain of the *Hannibal* thought of an expedient: cut off the heads of those who killed themselves – making sure that the captives were brought up on deck to witness the operation – and tell them that that suicide victims will return home without their heads. Others sought to commit suicide by simply refusing to eat. Some literally went mad. To counteract these responses, slavers soon developed a number of responses. Captives were forced-fed using a mouth opener to force the jaws apart. Food was then poured in via a funnel. More direct methods involved beating and using thumbscrews. No African, it seemed, could be allowed to die by his/her own will and intention. If he was going to die, it must be at the hand of his captors.

To avert the onset of many of the conditions identified above, slavers took to bringing Africans on upper deck in good weather, sometimes for exercise. As part of the exercise routine, captives would be forced to dance, and whipped when they refused. 'Whipping into cheerfulness' was prescribed as a therapeutic measure against suicidal melancholy. African captives were also told to sing.

The conditions that prevailed during bad weather when all hatches were closed and Africans confined to holds that could not be cleaned out provided the ideal breeding ground for epidemics. In 1838, the *Aquila Vengadora* arrived in Havana having lost 360 of the 560 Africans because of the need to close the hatches during bad weather.

Disease was not a risk that was covered by an insurance policy. Underwriters refused to issue such policies arguing that they would encourage captains to reduce the care provided to Africans. Indeed, shipowners might seek to make a profit out of insurance. The most notorious case of this dilemma was that faced by Captain Collingwood of *The Zong*.

THE *ZONG* MASSACRE

After leaving the coast of Africa in September 1781 with 470 captured Africans on board – more than the slave ship could hold – navigational error and bad weather extended the journey to four months, twice as long as normal. Three months into the journey 60 Africans had died, and many more looked as if they would. Dead captives represented a financial loss. It occurred to the captain, Luke Collingwood, that, with Africans treated as cargo with an insurance tag of £30 each, he could claim on the insurance for his losses, but not if they died from natural causes. Between 29th November and 1st December 1781, he therefore ordered his crew to throw over board the sickest captives and, if asked later, to say that the act had been necessary to safeguard the limited water supplies. When the Zong finally landed in Jamaica it still had 420 gallons of water on board, but 133 captive Africans had been drowned. Having learned of the presence of the water, and that Captain Collingwood had had opportunity to augment his stock from rainfall, the insurers refused to pay out and the case went to court twice in 1783, not over the murder of the Africans but to settle the insurance dispute. No officers or crew were charged with or prosecuted for murder. The case received a lot of attention in the press and was used by abolitionists to highlight the horrendous treatment of Africans. The judgment of the Solicitor-General, John Lee, offers one of the clearest expressions of the fundamental evil and inhumanity of the system. It confirmed too, the widely held belief and practice that Europeans had a power of death over Africans, and that African life was unworthy of life. We shall return to this point at the end.

Sometimes storms led to the immediate and dramatic loss of African life. In 1706, the Danish slave ship, *Kron Printzen*, sank with the loss of 820 Africans. In 1738 the Dutch slave ship, *Leuden*, sank with the loss of over 700 Africans after the crew had locked the hatches and abandoned ship. When the journey across the Atlantic Ocean became extended because of storms or lack of wind, captains were often forced to ration food and water. When rationing no longer sufficed, Africans would be asked to 'walk the plank'. French vessels were said to carry poisons for such eventualities.

INSURRECTIONS

The metal restraints and constant surveillance made insurrections difficult but not improbable. Records exist that document nearly 500 shipboard insurrections. Many more went undocumented. It was not in the interest of captains that publicity about insurrections should get out to owners and underwriters. Any captain whose voyages were plagued by insurrections would be perceived as either careless or as someone who could not handle Africans and keep mortality down.

The attention given to the endeavours of Sengbe Pieh (Cinque) in taking control of the schooner, *La Amistad*, in 1839, as a number of Africans were being

> 'What is the claim that human people have been thrown overboard? This is a case of chattels or goods. Blacks are goods and property: it is madness to accuse these well-serving honourable men of murder. They acted out of necessity and the most appropriate manner for the cause. The late Captain Collingwood acted in the interest of his ship to protect the safety of his crew. To question the judgement of an experienced well travelled captain held in the highest regard is one of folly, especially when talking of slaves. The case is the same as if horses had been thrown overboard.'

John Lee, Solicitor-General in the case of the *Zong*, 1783.

Slave ship crew firing upon rebellious African captives off coast of Gorée Island. Some leap overboard. Carl Wadström, *An Essay on Colonisation*, 1794-5. British Library Board. All rights reserved 065432.

moved from the Havana slave market to plantations elsewhere in Cuba, has overshadowed the long history of shipboard insurrections going back to 1539 when 190 Africans aboard the Portuguese ship, *Misericordia* ('Mercy'), revolted and killed all crew except two navigators who were forced to turn the boat around and take them back to Africa. In 1750, Africans aboard the *King David*, a Bristol slave ship bound for St Kitts, masterminded a plot to get access to the ships weapons and successfully take over the ship. Critical to the planning was an awareness of the reduction in crew size as a result of illness and death. Well into Caribbean waters at the time of the revolt, the undoing of the Africans was their inability to find a safe isolated place where the ship could anchor. After two weeks searching for a safe anchor, the French sent a sloop with 100 men to capture the *King David*.

Mortality amongst crew undoubtedly created favourable conditions for insurrection on many other ships. Indeed, there are instances when, because of death or incapacity, captains drafted in Africans to fill the void. Such was the situation of the Danish slave ship, *Fredensborg* in 1768. With twelve crewmen dead and a number of others sick, Captain Ferentz drafted in nine African captives as deck hands. Below deck, Africans from the Akwamu people of Ghana planned a revolt to take over the ship. Their struggle for freedom was, however, still-born when the plan was reported to the captain by an African crew member, Aye. The occasional use of Africans as crew members is only now being discussed within the literature.

The relative freedom that women and children had to move about the slave ship made them an important element in any plan to take over a ship. In the description of an attempted revolt that took place aboard the ship that was took him from Ghana to Grenada, Ottobah Cuguano confirmed this role of women and children.

The putting down of insurrections generally entailed much bloodshed. The punishment meted out to rebels was extreme. Captains resorted to thumbscrews, red-hot pokers, the severing of limbs, strangling, drowning and murder.

Faced with insurrections, European nations would put aside their competitive differences to lend each other a hand. Such was the situation recounted by William Richardson when a British ship went to the assistance of French slave ship from Nantes anchored off Bonny (Nigeria) that was about to sail. Sensing that this was their last opportunity for a successful revolt, Africans on board the ship rose and took over the deck.

'...when we found ourselves at last taken away, death was more preferable than life; and a plan was concerted amongst us, that we might burn and blow up the ship, and to perish altogether in the flames... It was the women and boys who were to burn the ship, with the approbation and groans of the rest; though that was prevented, the discovery was likewise a cruel bloody scene.'

Ottobah Cuguano,
Thoughts & Sentiments on the Evil of Slavery, 1787.

'I could not but admire the courage of a fine young black who, though his partner in irons lay dead at his feet, would not surrender but fought...until a ball finished his existence. The others fought as well as they could but what could they do against firearms? When they retreated to the forecastle...everyone that was able jumped overboard. By this time boats were coming from other ships to our assistance...to pick them up; but saved only one out of the whole number. Whether they died voluntarily, or were taken down by the sharks, we could not tell...the slaves below were in a mutiny knocking off their irons as fast as they could; but our captain...knew how to manage them with the least danger to us. Seeing an old sail on deck that the Frenchmen had been repairing, he ordered us to cover over the gratings with it and then knock the scuttles in close on each side of the ship to prevent the air from getting in...this done, we loaded our muskets with powder, but instead of shot we filled the barrels with cayenne pepper, which is plentiful here; then fired off through the gratings...and in a few minutes there was stench enough from the burnt pepper to almost suffocate them. This was the finishing blow; they cried out for mercy...led up two at a time and properly secured again.'

William Richardson, *A Mariner of England*, 1908.

THE MIDDLE PASSAGE AFTER BRITISH SLAVE TRADE ABOLITION IN 1807

The British Slave Trade Abolition Act of 1807 meant nothing for Africans transported across the Middle Passage. No African was freed to return to his/her town/village in Africa. The trafficking across the Atlantic Ocean was carried on by other nations, most notably by the Spanish and Portuguese, with the result that a further 3-4 million Africans entered the Americas during the nineteenth century. The transformation of the British Royal Navy from poacher to gamekeeper seemed in some instances to further imperil the lives of Africans as the countries still trafficking in Africans sought to adopt ocean-going vessels such as schooners and brigs which were not adapted to carrying people but could outrun Royal Navy frigates guarding the African coast. Vessels were more hideously over-crowded than ever and no attention was paid to the regulation of five men to two tons. Every method of economy was resorted to in order to lighten the ship, yet cram more captive Africans in. Accommodation space was diminished, and the amount of water and provisions reduced. A fraudulent device adopted by shipowners to get away with overcrowding was to register the vessel as of larger tonnage than it actually was. Such was the case of the Portuguese vessel, *Diana*, which held a royal licence for a 120-ton ship able to carry 300 Africans in 1824. When captured, the ship was found to be only 60 tons, a ratio of five men to one ton.

There were instances when, anticipating the capture and impounding of his ship, the captain would jettison his cargo. Such was the case of the brig, *Brillante*. Finding his brig surrounded by four patrolling cruisers, Captain Homans proceeded to attach the 600 manacled captives being transported to the anchor chain. When the cruisers lowered boats in order to board the *Brillante*, the anchor was thrown overboard carrying with it every man, woman and child. When the *Brillante* was boarded, all evidence had been removed of the trafficking.

THE MIDDLE PASSAGE AS AN EXPRESSION OF EUROPEAN DOMINATION

The overview presented above suggests the need for a deeper understanding of the Middle Passage, and the particular role played by the slave ship in the crime that was committed against Africans. The slave ship was an economic, and social-political system. Economically, the journey of a slave ship represented a significant financial undertaking. The cost of building and fitting out a ship, procuring the cargo to be exchanged for Africans, paying officers and crew, and securing insurance represented a huge investment whose risks were often shared out between a number of investors. The Africans transported represented the valuable cargo that was expected to yield a significant return on that investment, and make the fortunes of individuals involved in the trafficking. The profit and loss imperative reigned supreme, and governed the manner in which Africans were treated as chattel during the crossing.

The slave ship was also a socio-political system composed of a captain – who was chief executive, paymaster, camp-commandant and disciplinarian all rolled into one – supported by cast of officers and crew men whose singular purpose was to deliver the captured Africans to markets throughout the Americas and the Caribbean. Management of the slave ship required a panoply of technologies of discipline – chains, whips, bilboes, manacles, thumbscrews, red-hot pokers and mouth pincers. It also required technologies of surveillance such as sentinels

African slave traders throw sick and 'difficult-to-sell' Africans overboard near Port of Rio (Brazil) to avoid paying duties. Woodcut, 1832.

Opposite page: La rebellion d'un esclave sur un navire negrier, Edward Renard, 1833. Musée du Nouveau Monde, La Rochelle. Courtesy of Lief Svalesen.

THREE CONTINENTS, ONE HISTORY

and spies, as well as the imposition of no-go areas aboard ship. All of these technologies transformed the ship into a floating prison. Their singular aim was to neuter the freedom aspirations of the desperate people imprisoned in the holds who were willing to fight to the death to avoid the fate which their imagination conjured up.

Slave ship captains lived in constant fear and threat of insurrections, and the political ordering and governance of African life necessitated that violence should cascade downwards from the very top: from captain to officers, to sailors, and to the African captives. Violence was not a by-product of the trafficking in Africans; it was the handmaiden of power, and the founding principle of a system designed to transform Africans into docile

> '…Enormities frequently committed in an African ship…are considered…a matter of course. When the women and girls are taken on board a ship, naked, trembling, terrified, perhaps almost exhausted with cold, fatigue, and hunger, they are often exposed to the wanton rudeness of white savages…where resistance or refusal would be utterly in vain, even the solicitation of consent is seldom thought of.'
>
> John Newton,
> *The Journal of a Slave Trader, 1750-54.*

Right: Captain Kimber of the British slave ship *Recovery*, punishing a Nigerian girl who had refused to dance naked on the deck of the ship. Engraved coloured print by George Cruikshank.

spirits and automata that responded only when touched by the whip. Every aspect of everyday life had to legitimise this equation between violence, power and authority. Not only were sailors permitted to use violence against African captives, but they were actively encouraged to do so. No area of slave-ship life expresses this more directly than the rape and sexual violation of women and children.

As on Caribbean plantations, slave ships came to be seen as a porno-tropic space where every sexual fantasy could be realised without opprobrium or countervailing influence. Rape and sexual violation had no real consequences for the perpetrator. African women seemed to exist only for the pleasure of the crew. This was reflected in the allusion to women's quarters on Dutch ships as the *hoeregat*, or whorehouse. The outcome of this sexual licence is that thousands of female captives arrived pregnant in the Americas.

All acts of aggression and violence were part of the larger political ordering of life aboard slave ship. By being routinised and normalised, they allowed the perpetrators to develop shields that desensitised them from grasping the horror and dehumanisation inflicted upon their victims. This is what Falconbridge referred to as the omnipresent callousness: "the common practice of the officers in the Guinea trade…justify the assertion, that to harden to feelings, and to inspire a delight in giving torture to a fellow creature, is the natural tendency."

The irony is that the majority of those who inflicted the worst degradations were themselves degraded. Two things explained this conundrum: (a) identity, and (b) security. In relation to the first, it was precisely in the act of degrading Africans and placing the latter outside the universe of obligation within which moral questions have to be asked, that white sailors came to assert their own sense of being free, white men. More than that, their perception of themselves as free, white men seemed to be contingent on the domination exercised over Africans.

The security issue was also an identity issue. What the identification as 'free' and 'white' achieved, despite the murderous floggings and general maltreatment that white seamen experienced at the hands of ship's captains, was that it allowed ordinary white sailors to be made over on to the side of those who could be trusted, i.e. on 'our' side, on the side of the master. The ambivalence of the identification always had to be shored up by reinforcing the perception of Africans as different and as a threat. Thus goaded, the captain would have more assurance of the perpetual vigilance of his crew in spotting every minutiae of a possible plot such as secret signs and the look of hatred in the eyes of Africans.

The carceral regime governing the African aboard slave ships both extended the treatment that African captives had already been exposed to in the factories, forts and barracoons on the African coast and prepared them for the plantation world awaiting them on disembarkation in the Americas and the Caribbean.

> 'It was common for the filthy sailors to take the African women and lie upon their bodies.'
>
> Ottobah Cuguano,
> *Thoughts & Sentiments on the Evil of Slavery*, 1787.

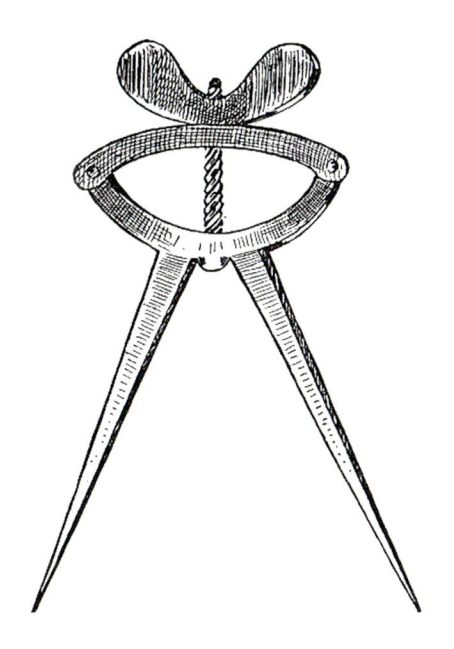

Above: Mouth vise used to force feed African captives who preferred to starve themselves to death.

4

Slavery and Emancipation

Dr Clive Harris

The manner in which the British 1807 Abolition of the Slave Trade has been marked in bicentenary celebrations has exposed the varied understandings that prevail about the nature of the slave system established in the Caribbean by Europeans. For some it was understood in term of the unparalleled horror of the experience. For others, Caribbean slavery can be yoked to other forms of unfree and bonded labour. This was a feature of many exhibitions and their desire to be inclusive. Sometimes this yoking has been an expression of an explicit or implicit politics that says that it is better to focus on and address contemporary forms of unfree labour and leave behind those of the past that we can no longer correct. The irony is that these contemporary manifestations examined seemed to map on to those places from which Africans were taken by Europeans over a period of 400 years.

Any approach to understanding slavery by generalising a least common denominator such as unfree or bonded labour as the unifying characteristic of all slave systems, irrespective of time or place, is always going to be an unsatisfactory scholarship. It suggests, for example, that there was a certain equation between the situation of white indentured workers and the situation of enslaved Africans on New World plantations.

DEFINING ELEMENT OF CARIBBEAN SLAVERY
The defining element of Caribbean slavery that sets it apart from earlier forms of enslavement was the motive or purpose: making money or, more accurately, making a profit on the investment of money. A notion of chattel slavery which focuses only on the commodification of people, and the brutality of this transformation of people into things, will always fall short unless it simultaneously connects it with the profit motive. Africans were forcibly removed from their homes in Africa and transported across the Atlantic to a place they had never seen in order to make money/profit for Europeans. When we use the phrase money/profit we are not talking about the smash and grab efforts that marked the conquest and plunder of the Aztec and the Inca empires that enabled Spanish conquistadores to seize the wealth of the region. We are talking about a sustained commitment to financial investment in mining and agriculture over a long period of time. The Jamaican historian, Bryan Edwards, in the

late eighteenth century, estimated that an average plantation with a labour force of 250 Africans making 200 hogsheads of sugar required a capital outlay in the region of £30,000 sterling.

With the virtual extermination of the native population in large areas of the Caribbean basin, Europeans had to find an alternative answer to the region's labour problem. It found the solution in the blueprint that had been developed by the Portuguese long before Columbus sailed for the Americas, in the sugar plantations of the Canary Islands, Sao Tome and the Cape Verde islands utilising enslaved Africans. This model was transplanted to Brazil and other parts of the Caribbean.

ON THE PLANTATION

At the top of plantation structure were Europeans. In British territories, they were not homogeneous. In the key sugar island of Jamaica, the dominant European group was stratified between English owners, Scottish managers and Irish overseers. By the end of the eighteenth century the majority of English owners had become absentee landlords who generally left their estates in the hands of managers, often called attorneys (nothing to do with law) who might be charged with managing sometimes as many as 40 estates. Alongside these one might find proprietors of small estates (mainly coffee and indigo), sometimes a stepping stone used by managers into plantation ownership proper. In the latter years of slavery, some of these owners were Jewish, 'mixed' or 'coloured'.

Amongst the enslaved, there were a number of social divisions, the most significant being that between those who worked in the field, in the manufacturing process and in the Great House administering to the personal needs of the white owner. In field labour, the division of labour was based on physical strength. The buying and selling of Africans on the basis of physical stamina led to the emergence of a racist folklore among plantation owners about the stereotypical characteristics of the different African peoples ranked exclusively in relation to their economic potential for the plantation system: the Ashanti were reputedly strong but rebellious; the Igbos more 'docile' but cunning and deceitful, etc, etc.

Field slaves were generally divided into three,

Planting sugar cane on Bodkins Estate, Antigua. William Clarke, *Ten Views in the Island of Antigua*, 1823. British Library Board. All rights reserved 062474.

> 'It was more the object of the overseers to work the slaves out, and trust for supplies from Africa... I have heard many overseers say:
> "I have made my employer 20, 30, 40 more hogsheads per year than any of my predecessors ever did; and though I have killed 30 or 40 negroes per year more, yet the produce has been more than adequate to that loss"'.
>
> **Henry Coor, evidence to House of Common Select Committee on Slave Trade, 1790-91.**

Interior of a boiling house. William Clarke, *Ten Views in the Island of Antigua*, 1823. British Library Board. All rights reserved 004307.

sometimes four, gangs. The first gang was composed of able-bodied men and women plus about three drivers (enslaved Africans who supervised the workers with whips) and two cooks. The second gang was composed of youths, 14-18 year old (boys and girls), pregnant women after four months and partial invalids. They were accompanied by one driver and two cooks. The third gang was composed of girls and boys aged 9-14, old women and women close to child birth. They were generally accompanied by a driveress and two cooks. On many estates there was generally a subsidiary gang called the 'pickaninny' gang composed of children aged 4-8 years old under the supervision of a matron. For the planter it was important that from an early age these children should become inured to the plantation regime by attending the morning musters and performing useful labour such as cutting grass.

The manufacturing process – and it must be remembered that each estate at this time had its own factory – was organised not on a gang basis but on the basis of technique. Mill workers were divided into boiler-men, syphon-men, stokers, etc. These positions tended to be male dominated. In addition to these factory workers, there was another group of labourers who existed effectively outside the cultivation and manufacturing process, i.e. the tradesmen such as masons, coopers, blacksmiths and carpenters. These were not necessarily slaves and were quite often 'coloured' or also white secured on a wage basis in order to preserve the legal ratio of one white to ten blacks.

Between the planter class and enslaved Africans were those who were responsible for the day-to-day management and control of estates: overseers and bookkeepers. The overseer managed the estate and took responsibility for ensuring that the whole thing came together to make the owner a profit. He was assisted by a book-keeper, who contrary to the nomenclature, never saw a book in his life. The latter's role was fundamentally disciplinary. Armed with long and short whips, he would physically accompany enslaved Africans in the field and in the sugar mill. In this labour of direct supervision, the bookkeeper was assisted by a black headman or driver. Together, the bookkeeper and the various drivers performed the function of non-commissioned officers who regimented and disciplined the workers to exact the maximum amount of effort. The enslaved African, wrote one Jamaican planter, was an 'automaton that moved when touched by the whip'.

The complex system of domination and discipline that was put in place for encouraging habitual labour and extracting the maximum effort from workers ensured that of the 100 slaves who left the coast of Africa, only 84 reached the West Indies, and of these one third had died within three years. To put it another way, for every 56 on plantations at the end of three years, 44 had perished. Underpinning this level of mortality was the fundamental economic principle that there wa no need for the planter to economise labour. A rational capitalist accounting suggested that it was better to work the African to death within seven or eight years and trust to the market to replace him/her. This was the understanding of Henry Coor, who had worked as a millwright on a Jamaica estate for fifteen years.

The logic of this economic rationale is that once the slave trade was abolished the African population declined in all territories except the United States. In Jamaica this decline continued until about 1820 despite the measures adopted by planters to encourage Africans to have more children such as time off for women.

DOMINATION AND THE PURSUIT OF PROFIT

One often finds euphemistic phrases like 'Africans were reduced to slavery'. Africans were not reduced to slavery. Rather Europeans constructed a bureaucratic and paramilitary chain of social relationships which started in the African forts, continued on the slave ships, and intensified on the Caribbean plantation which aimed to transform rebel spirits into docile creatures from sun-up till sun down, and sometimes beyond sun-down. The overriding aim of what was called 'the seasoning process' – the first three years of adjustment – was to break the will of the African. 'Seasoning' was nothing less than the domination that planters sought to exercise.

Domination in turn was the expression of a power relationship that was social, physical, cultural, psychological and sexual. Socially, the aim of the system was to deny the African a legitimate social existence and human rights outside of the master/slave relationship. Access to property such as land was subject to the power of the master. Until 1816 this power was supreme. There was no appeal to an ombudsman or to a magistrate. Each plantation was a self-sufficient institution that had its own House of Correction, its own hospital and medical personnel for providing what was deemed to be appropriate medical treatment, and for making and declaring people fit for work. Children were separated from their mothers and placed in creches supervised by a nannies while their mothers laboured in the field. There was no possibility of an enslaved person bringing an action for personal injury done to him/her. It remained for the owner to prosecute by indicating how the personal injury done to his property deprived him of, or rendered less valuable, the service of his worker/capital. Until 1826, the evidence of an enslaved African was not admissible as evidence unless accompanied by a certificate of baptism. As the law stood, enslaved Africans were competent witnesses only against other Africans or maroons.

Social domination was exemplified by attempts to strip the African of his/her cultural heritage. The symbolic stripping of the African's name and the imposition of a substitute name that seemed at times to inversely correlate with the African's degradation, was the first step in this process. An entry in the St Kitts Slave Register of 1817 in which a fourteen-year old young man is described as having the name of Nobody expresses this total disrespect for the African.

> 'When his place can at once be supplied from foreign preserves, the duration of his life becomes a matter of less moment than its productiveness while it lasts. It is accordingly a maxim of slave management, in slave importing countries, that the most effective economy is that which takes out of the human chattel in the shortest space of time the utmost amount of exertion it is capable of putting forth. It is in tropical culture, where annual profits often equal the whole capital of plantations, that Negro life is most recklessly sacrificed. It is the agriculture of the West Indies…that has engulfed millions of the African race.'
>
> **Karl Marx,** *Das Kapital,* **vol.1.**

Below: A Surinam planter in his morning dress. A femal slave in the background, pouring a drink. British Library Board. All rights reserved 004310.

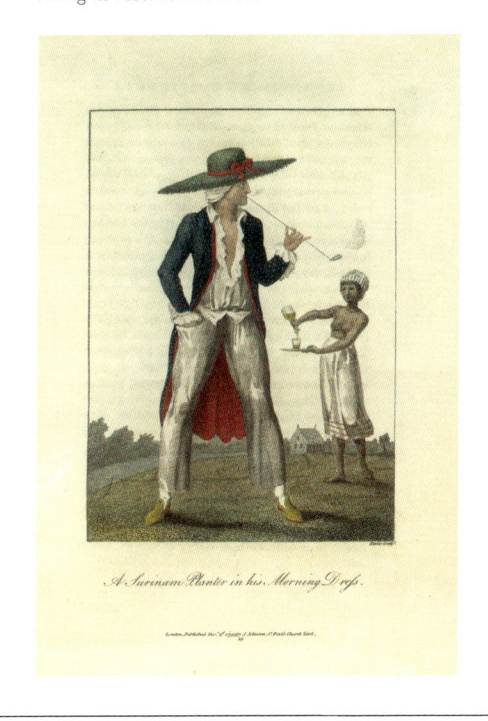

> 'Whereas divers large estate...have from time to time been left by white persons to mulattoes and other the offspring of mulattoes not being their own issue born in lawful wedlock. And whereas such bequests tend greatly to destroy the distinction requisite, and absolutely necessary to be kept up in this island, between white persons and negroes...be it therefore enacted...that from and after the first day of January, 1752, no lands, negro, mulatto, or other slaves, cattle stock, money, or other real or personal estate...shall be given... or declared to be in trust for...or devised by any white person to any negro whatsoever, or to any mulatto, or other person, not being their own issue born in lawful wedlock and being the issue of a Negro'.
>
> **1751 Jamaican Act.**

African field worker with neck collar being flogged by white book-keeper. British Library Board. All rights reserved 062469.

Name	Sex	Colour	Age	Birth
Venus	Female	Black	6 months	Ditto
Nobody	Male	Black	14 years	Ditto

In this Register, enslaved Africans are not allowed a surname that might speak of roots and ancestry. The denial of language and culture more generally reaffirmed this attempt to separate the African from ties of birth or roots. This separation was reinforced in a denial of a claim to the future as reflected in rights over children who could arbitrarily be separated from parents at the whim of the master, as could an individual's partner.

Psychologically, the disciplinary regime of the plantation aimed to create a relationship of dependency on the master which operated at the level of language and manners/etiquette. Take, for example, the case where every enslaved adult and child, on the pain of punishment or worse, had to call every white child, 'Miss' or 'Master', and had to adopt the obsequious practice of doffing their hats/caps to passing white persons, flashing 'massa' a smile to convince him that all was well in his world, refusing eye contact for fear of being deemed 'uppity', or moving off pavements in the towns to allow white persons to pass by. In short, to make oneself socially insignificant.

In the porno-tropics of the plantation where unbridled sexual licence for the master was de rigueur and where a charge of rape could never be brought, it was perceived as the 'greatest disgrace' (Henry Coor) for any white man not to have sexual relations with those whom he commanded. Conversely, for many enslaved women, such relations were sometimes perceived as a route to social advancement and better treatment for self and children. On the plantation there was no need to discipline the bodies of white men and repress desires. What mattered was not the regulation of sex but the regulation of the status of the mixed children that resulted in order to preserve the necessary distinction between white and black. European slave codes stated that children, mixed or not, assumed the legal status of their mothers at birth. i.e. they were slaves. In situations where fathers chose not to respect this practice, the response was measures such as the 1751 Jamaican Act which limited the value of the property that could be acquired under a will by 'persons of colour'. Under another act, it was categorically stated that where a white person left property to his 'coloured' children by deed or will, this property should be distributed among his legitimate next of kin as if he had died intestate. Persons of African descent not born in lawful wedlock were prohibited from purchasing property worth more than £2,000. Despite these varied measures, the 'mixing of blood', 'la mélange des sangs', came to be seen as a fundamental threat to social order.

Supporting all of these relations was the power of violence exercised by the master. Unlike Spanish and French territories which had their *Siete Partidas*, and *Code Noir* respectively, the first comprehensive legal provision in the English colonies did not appear until the Barbados Slave Code of 1661. This document became the model for other English territories in the Caribbean and in the United States of America. The English codes reflected the need for constant vigilance on the part of Europeans against Africans; and effectively legitimised a state of war between the two groups. They prescribed a graded list of punishments for every possible misdemeanour, with an increased tariff for repeat offenders. For minor offences such as lateness, insubordination and fighting, whipping, (indefinite) imprisonment, and the treadmill were seen as appropriate. For more serious offences such as running away and plotting rebellions (even when guilt was not established), the tariffs might include the loss of a limb, (public) torture, death, gibbeting, castration, dismemberment. If in the act of punishment, the enslaved African died, this was not deemed to be murder. For 'unprovoked' murder of an African, a European was fined £15. It was not until the beginning of the nineteenth century that there came into being a crime of murder against an African. The most common mode of punishment was the public whipping of the naked African body. The motive here was not only to punish but also to humiliate, and strip away any vestige of personal dignity. The

TREAD-WHEEL.

'Whatever distance they may be from their origin, they always keep the stain of slavery, and are declared incapable of all public functions. Even gentlemen who descends to any degree from a woman of color cannot enjoy the prerogatives of nobility. The law is harsh, but wise and necessary. In a country where there are fifteen slaves to one white, one cannot put too much distance between the two species, one cannot impress upon the blacks too much respect for those they serve. This distinction, rigorously observed even after freedom, is the principal prop of the subordination of the slave, by the opinion that results that his color is inextricably linked with servitude, and nothing can render him equal to his master...'

Memoire au Roi, quoted in Antoine Gisler, (1964) *L'Esclavage aux Antilles Francaises* **(XVIIe-XIXe siecles).**

Interior of a Jamaican House of Correction: Africans on Treadmill being flogged by black driver. British Library Board. All rights reserved 004306.

THREE CONTINENTS, ONE HISTORY

more the ratio between Africans and Europeans became more marked, the more extreme did these relationships of domination become.

Important though it is to describe the various technologies of domination adopted on plantations, there are two other aspects that should be addressed to achieve a proper understanding of slavery, namely, (a) attention to the phenomenon of super-ordination, and (b) the manner in which Africans kept alive their culture.

In relation to the first, there is a growing body of literature that talks at length about whiteness as a system of representation though which the colour white gets coded as other things. What is generally omitted is a discussion of white power as a system of super-ordination and dominance through which Europeans arrogated to themselves the benefits and privileges of slave society. Subordination and dominance necessarily went together. If the disciplinary regime sought to produce an individual who could occupy the box called 'slave', it equally sought to produce, and did produce, its opposite, an individual who was ready and willing to fill the box called 'master'. Being a master meant a whole range of things:

- A belief in the inherent right or power to command others
- A belief that he/she was at the centre of the universe, and that all the desires and wishes of the enslaved should to be expressed through him, i.e. the enslaved was dependent on him and should be grateful for this fact
- A right to expect the slave to produce for him and serve him materially and physically
- A right of access to the slave's body
- A paternalistic assumption of responsibility
- A right to discipline the slave, and, perhaps most important of all,
- A demand for recognition, a demand to be recognised as a (white) master.

The purpose of the slave codes was not merely to punish Africans for every infraction, but to produce the categories of master and slave locked into a binary system of superiorisation and inferiorisation. The Barbados Slave Code is full of what we would now call negative racist stereotypes: Africans were 'heathenish', 'brutal', 'a dangerous kind of people', with 'naturally wicked instincts', and have 'a barbarous, wild and savage nature'. In this context, racism had nothing to do with fear of strangers or outsiders, but had to do instead with the production of a permanent division between those who are deemed to be fit and unfit.

It is perhaps not accidental that all of these stereotypes became harnessed by the pseudo-scientific concepts of 'race' and 'species' that made their appearance just when the struggle between Europeans and Africans intensified in the late eighteenth century, i.e. when Africans struggled to assert their humanity using the language of 'Liberty, Equality and Fraternity' that Europeans were arrogating to themselves in their struggles against feudal inequality. By transforming the struggle between Africans and Europeans into a struggle between dominant and inferior race, notions of 'race' sought to create an unbridgeable chasm between self and other that led inexorably

'Chatiment des Quatres Piquets dans les Colonies' (Punishment of the Four Stakes/Pegs), painting Marcel Verdier (1849). The whipping of a fugitive slave by a black driver. As the most common form of punishment meted out to Africans, it was important that whipping should not only humiliate the offender but take the form of a public spectacle to deter others. Even the young white child had to understand from an early age what the disciplinary power of master/mistress entailed.
Source: Menil Foundation, Houston, Texas. Published in Hugh Honour, *The Image of the Black in Western Art* (1989).

'Interest and security demand that we overwhelm the black race with so much disdain that whoever descends from it until the sixth generation shall be covered by an indelible stain.'

Hilliard d'Auberteuil, *Considerations sur l'etat present de la colonies francaise de Saint Domingue*, 1776-77.

to the simple equation: white = free; black = slave. Colour, as a mark of difference, seemed to assign the individual to particular positions within the social structure that owed their origin not to historical crimes but to nature and biology. When history becomes biology, inequality became 'natural' and legitimate. Abolitionists might have conceded that it was wrong to enslave Africans but they never for one moment gave up the paternalistic right to tutor and save the African, and to expect gratitude for this tutelage.

However much the disciplinary regime of the plantation damaged the bodies of Africans, it did not damage their spirit and resilience. Crucial areas of the lives of enslaved Africans were largely outside of the disciplinary regime: the provision ground and the higglering that took place on the day set aside as market day, religion and some aspects of expressive culture. The role played by religion in the struggles for freedom is a testimony to this escape from the disciplinary regime. The threat posed by the retention of these practices were so well recognised that incoming missionaries devoted a lot of attention to erasing them.

APPRENTICESHIP

As it became absolutely clear that the fabric of slavery would never survive a repeat of the Sharpe Christmas Rebellion of 1831-32 in Jamaica, the British government moved swiftly to pass the 1833 Abolition of Slavery Act despite the howls and protests of the white owners. These howls were given their quietus by the offer of compensation to the tune of £20 million for the loss of ownership over Africans. (After four centuries of brutalisation, Africans got nothing.) The receipt of this compensation was made conditional on the passing of a number of ordinances relating to punishment, vagrancy, manumission, length of working week, housing, food, clothing and so on that laid the platform for the experiment that was to follow. Africans were declared legally free on 1st August 1834, but real freedom did not follow. What followed was a half-way house that became known as the Apprenticeship (1834-1838). Essentially what changed was that the power of the individual master was transformed into the power of the state. The state insisted that though supposedly 'free', Africans had to remain on the master's estate for a period of 4-6 years and do the same work as they had done before for 45 hours a week.

The Abolition Act made provision for adjudication by a body of stipendiary magistrates whose main duty was to monitor the system particularly in relation to the payment of wages for additional labour and the use of land. These magistrates were perceived as having an important role in teaching Africans about the essence of the new property relations. In other words, though he/she had been made 'free', other aspects of the planter's capital had not been similarly liberated: not the sugar cane, not the tools, not the land, and not the animals. They had to learn the distinction between *meum* and *tuum*, mine and yours. The estate House of Correction was replaced by a state penal system that was buttressed by a new Vagrancy Act, and measures designed to curtail the ability of Africans to acquire land independent of the plantation.

While coercion was clearly vital to the success of the Apprenticeship experiment, great store was also placed on the role of religion and religious education as midwives for the new society. A fund was set up to enable missionaries to proselytise without restriction, build churches and set up schools for those under six who were

> 'Although the negroes are now under a system of limited control, which secure to a certain extent their orderly and industrious conduct, in the short space of 5 years from the first of next August, their performance of the functions of a labouring class in a civilised community will depend entirely on the power over their minds in the same prudential and moral notions which govern more or less the mass of the people here (in Britain).'
>
> **Rev Stirling, West Indian Education.**

Carrying a Sedan Chair (Palanquin), Rio de Janeiro, Brazil, ca. 1770s. Source: Carlos Juliao, *Riscos illuminados de figurinhos de broncos e negros dos uzos do Rio de Janeiro e Serro do Frio* (Rio de Janeiro, 1960). An upper class woman being transported in her sedan chair by two slaves, each dressed in livery but barefoot.

automatically relieved of field labour. Rev Stirling who was charged with drawing up the blueprint for 'religious and moral education' was clear in his mind that Africans could not be allowed to retain the kind of 'dangerous traditions' which had led to the Haitian Revolution and the Christmas Rebellion. Africans might consider themselves free in Jesus but this inner freedom could never be externalised. For many planters religious and moral education was a waste of time and served only to spoil the African. This was the opinion of the planter mouthpiece, the *Kingston Chronicle*.

On August 1st 1838, the Apprenticeship came to and end, and the real struggles over labour and rent were to begin. In the colonies of other European nations, slavery remained in place: in French and Danish territories emancipation came in 1848; in Dutch territories, it came in 1863; in the Spanish territories which had not gained their independence during the Wars of Independence of the 1820s, it came in 1886; and in Brazil, which had been there from the beginning, the end came in 1888. Compensation was paid to all planters except those in Cuba.

LEGACIES

Healing the wounds of four centuries of European domination and the reduction of Africans to objects that could be used for making profit became a challenge faced by all societies that participated in this history. This challenge has been economic, political, social and psychological. The forcible transportation of Africans means that today 140 million Africans now live the Americas, where they compose one third of the population of the region. In none of the societies where slavery prevailed did the process of emancipation seek to empower Africans and compensate them such that they could take their place as full citizens in the new societies in which they now lived. The vision of freedom that was entertained by the architects of emancipation process was one in which White over Black was the agreed political formula. This explains why, since the ending of slavery, there has been an unabated struggle against the pervasive discrimination and racialised inequality which place Africans at the bottom rungs in many Latin American societies. In all societies, even those where Africans constitute the majority of the population, lives continue to be blighted by the social values laid down during slavery, particularly around issues of 'race' and 'colour'.

One of the most pernicious and debilitating legacies of Caribbean slave societies throughout the Americas was a profoundly race/colour consciousness or pigmentocracy, as reflected in terms like 'good'/'bad hair'; 'good/bad' complexion; 'nice' nose. A plethora of social types based on colour/race came into being in which Europeans, 'coloureds' and Africans were ranked according to their perceived racial qualities. In British colonies, a large number of gradations or categories were developed to define where on the continuum individuals could be placed: negro, sambo, mulatto, quadroon, mustee, mustiphini, quintroon, octoroon, white. In Spanish colonies there were more multitudinous categories reflecting the presence not only of Europeans and Africans but also native Americans. One way an individual could escape slavery was literally to breed out the 'African blood' over a series of generations – what an American visitor to Jamaica in 1850 call the 'great stampede whitewards'. While many of the gradations have been somewhat attenuated, the broad racialised divisions still prevail. In the minds

---

'We are sickened by the daily doses of unmeaning twaddle repeated ad nauseam as to the moral and religious instruction of the people being the only means of restraining the idle and vicious habits of the Negroes, and promoting the welfare of the country. Now any person who has discrimination to observe accurately the progress of the passing events must perceive that there is no lack of teachers and preachers of all sorts, colours, and sects, nor of crowded congregations to listen to their moral and religious instructions – and yet, the population now at liberty to preach and pray as much as they please, are every day becoming more licentious and corrupt! Not a vessel arrives without a fresh importation of preachers, psalm-books and Bibles. There are chapels and meeting houses in every corner of the city. The Negroes neglect all household duties to attend them…. Religion is like liberty – it cannot be conferred on those incapable of appreciating its value…. Everything for their souls – nothing for their bodies…. Instead of being taught the mechanical arts, the use of the plough and harrow, the plane and the adze, the awl or needle…. Instead of practical industry, temperance and integrity, they are taught to read Bibles and sing hymns. They all begin at the wrong end. They attempt to finish the superstructure before they have laid the foundations.'

Kingston Chronicle, 3 November 1835.

of abolitionists, anti-slavery did not require anti-racism.

Even the beacon of light that burned 200 years ago in the Haitian Revolution seems barely to flicker today against a background of grinding poverty. European countries worked in concert with the United States to ensure that the Haitian Republic had to recognise French demands for compensation for loss of property in the island. Under the weight of international diplomatic pressure, the Haitians eventually capitulated in 1825 and agreed to pay France compensation of 150 million gold francs. It took the country 100 years to redeem this indemnity. The repayments bled the national treasury dry.

In recent years, there has been increasing interest in examining what are perceived as psychological scars of slavery that have not been healed. The trauma of enslavement is said to be partly responsible for the aberrant, self-destructive, and fratricidal behaviour of young men involved in guns and gangs. The work of Joy deGruy Leary (Post Traumatic Slave Syndrome) comes to mind here. To my mind, this is something of an ahistorical over-simplification in that it ignores the pernicious impact of the system that replaced slavery in most societies and has continued up to the present. The key feature of the post-emancipation era was that its focus was not so much the *body* of the African but the *mind* of the African. William Ewart Gladstone understood this well when he proceeded to draft the blueprint for the new post-slavery society. We are removing their physical shackles, he stated, we must shackle their minds. The outcome was a massive missionary onslaught designed to give Africans Christianity and take away at the same time their 'dangerous' religious traditions in which Gods demanded vengeance rather than submission and the turning of the other cheek.

Another area that requires a lot more research is the individualism that the new society sought to inculcate in the African to counter the collectivism that had allowed many to survive slavery. The Baptists, above all missionary societies, launched an onslaught against what they called the 'herd instinct'. Motivated by the principle of voluntaryism, parents were encouraged to assume responsibility for paying the pences necessary for the construction and upkeep of the church whose ownership was lodged with the London HQ, the education provided to their children, and the stipend received by those who administered to their souls. The establishment of 'free villages' was meant to encourage this process. By and large, however, most denominations, preferred to make an accommodation with the system and saw no need to challenge the dependency culture that planters had tried to instil in Africans, particularly through the system of 'indulgences' provided by the master. Today, the twin problem of individualism and dependency is one that bedevils the African-Caribbean community in Britain.

The Voice of Liberty

'The Good Lord who created the sum gives us light from above, who rouses the sea and makes the thunder roar – listen well, all of you – this god, hidden in the clouds, watches us. He sees all that the white man does. The god of the white man calls him to commit crimes: our god asks only good works of us. But this god who is so good orders revenge! He will direct our hands; he will aid us. Throw away the image of the god of the whites who thirsts for our tears and listen to the voice of liberty which speaks in the hearts of all of us.'

Boukman Dutty, quoted in Carolyn Fick (1990), *The Voice of Haiti.*

5

Resistance

Dr Clive Harris

Armed Maroon, Surinam, 1770s, from *Narrative of a Five Years Expedition Against the Revolted Negroes of Surinam* © The Atlantic Slave Trade and Slave Life in the Americas: A Visual Record.

If the central focus given to humanitarianism in the 2007 bicentenary of the Abolition of the Slave Trade seemed to intimate that the desire for freedom came from without rather than from within, this chapter provides an alternative reading that suggests that the real desire and struggle for freedom came from the Africans themselves. Africans caught up in the trafficking across the Middle Passage had no desire to be enslaved, and resisted at every turn the illegal imposition of European enslavement. Resistance to the trafficking and slavery covered a broad spectrum of activities. Armed revolt was only one extreme of a continuum which stretched from satire, lying, feigning illness and working slow, to tool-breaking, theft, running away, strikes, self-mutilation, suicide/dirt-eating, infanticide, arson, and poisoning. Much of the academic scholarship on resistance has tried to make sense the phenomenon by distinguishing between 'true resistance' – overt and communal – and 'intransigence' (individual, sporadic and clandestine), or between violent and passive resistance or even between 'inward' and 'outward' resistance. Imputing motive to actions post hoc, when the historical traces and the terminology that come down to us are almost invariably European, makes that sort of exercise extremely problematic. What can be said categorically, is that Africans resisted at every stage of the process of enslavement: (1) at the point of capture and sale, (2) in transit to the coast, (3) in the factory forts and barracoons, (4) on board slave ships, and (5) on plantations in the Americas. Space prevents us from covering each of these arenas in equal depth. The first three arenas we shall address under the more general topic of Resistance in Africa.

RESISTANCE IN AFRICA

It is now an accepted fact that, without the willing or unwilling support of many African kings, nobles, and merchants, the trafficking in Africans across the Atlantic would not have reached the scale that it did. Important kingdoms such as Dahomey, Congo, Oyo, and the Ashanti Federation over a period of time were drawn into a web of alliances that led them to wage war against their neighbours for the sole purpose of accumulating wealth through the provision of captives to Europeans. Client states of this kind sprang up in the vicinity of the protective perimeter of coastal forts. As slave raiding ventured deeper into the interior of the continent, African states a long way from the coast such as the Bambara State of Segu restructured themselves as "enormous machines for producing slaves". Some states, such as Congo and Benin, which had expressed early opposition to the trafficking, were soon drawn into a network of trafficking alliances.

The complicity of certain African rulers in this crime against humanity has often overshadowed the resistance to the trafficking by other African rulers, the general African population who were always in danger of being enslaved themselves, and by the captured Africans themselves. It is important therefore that one should make a clear separation between the interests of states that allowed themselves to be incorporated into a slave system, and the interest of free peoples who were under constant threat of enslavement.

The initial attempts by Europeans to build forts on the coast of Africa often encountered strong resistance when the actions of Europeans moved from trading in commodities such as gold, gum Arabic and palm oil to trafficking in people. Armed soldiers were needed to supervise the construction of the Danish fort of Prinzsten near Keta in eastern Ghana to ward off attacks from the local Ewe people. Even when such forts were built under the overlordship of local rulers to whom rent was paid, the opposition remained strong. Sometimes a local leader might support one European nation but not another.

The constant exposure to raids from professional warriors often moved ordinary people to act in solidarity with those who were already captured. Hard evidence of such action can be found in the insurance records of Lloyd's List which shows that in more than 17 percent of cases of damage to vessels, the damage was due to local rebellions by the captives themselves, sometimes aided by the coastal population.

In what is now Senegal the attempts by local rulers to enslave and sell their own people gave rise, at the end of the seventeenth century, to the Marabout War and Toubenan movement (from the word *tuub*, meaning to convert to Islam). Further south in Angola, the Kongo population, following the preaching of Kimpa Vita (see below,) invoked Christianity in the same way, both against missionaries compromised by the trafficking, and against the manikongo (King) and his nobles.

The analysis of the records of the English African Company reveals how common incidents of protests and rebellions were at their various forts/factories on the West African coast. In 1758 a Liverpool slave ship, the *Perfect*, captained by William Potter, which was completing the purchase of 300 Africans on River Gambia, was attacked by members of the local community who killed the entire crew. In Nigeria, a French vessel from Bordeaux, the *Cote d'or*, was similarly attacked by warriors in a rafts on the River Bonny. Heavily armed with guns and knives, the warriors boarded the ship and freed the captives. The crew managed to escape with their life because an English vessel arrived.

Within the forts/factories that processed Africans for the Middle Passage, eyewitness accounts survive that reveal that Africans took every opportunity to free themselves. In 1703 Africans overpowered the guards at the Royal African Company's fort at Sekondi and beheaded its governor. At the Dutch fort of Christiansborg in 1727, African captives succeeded in organising a rebellion in which the governor of the fort was killed. Most escaped.

Le Negre Marron (The Black Maroon) in Creole, 'Neg Mawon'), Port-au-Prince, Haiti, often translated in English as the statue of the 'Unknown Slave'. The Negre Marron is shown with left leg extended (broken chain on his ankle); a machete in his right hand, and his left hand holding a conch shell to his lips. The conch shell was often used as a trumpet to assemble people. Created by the Haitian sculptor, Albert Mangones, the statue was commissioned to commemorate the slaves who revolted against France from 1791 to 1804.

Those who could not get away, because of factors such as injury, were made an example of when Europeans recovered the fort. All were put to death, beheaded and thrown into the sea, as was the norm.

In Chapter 3, we have explored the possibilities that were available to Africans to rebel aboard the slave ship. These possibilities varied between national slave ship owners. For example, in contrast to Dutch ships where the insurrection rate was one in every eighteen journeys; on board French vessels it was one in fifteen voyages. Most attempts at insurrection tended to take place when the ship was still relatively close to the African coast.

In the Americas, resistance took a number of forms. Damage to property was common. Stealing the master's provisions and livestock was also prevalent. Charles Small, an ex-slave, believed that no enslaved African "believed he had violated any rule of morality by appropriating to himself anything that belonged to his master, if it was necessary to his comfort." In other words, he was merely helping the master to preserve the value of the African as capital. Feigning illness was a common method for avoiding work. Matthew 'Monk' Lewis report in 1817 that 45 of his 300 slaves reported to the hospital claiming what the plantation medical staff called false ailments and pains, in order to avoid gruelling field labour.

At an individual level, suicide was common. So too was infanticide. Women often found ways of killing their unborn child to prevent them from being born into slavery. From the moment that Africans first arrived in the Americas, running away has represented one of the strategies used by Africans for dealing with the environment in which they found themselves. Over four centuries, thousands of enslaved Africans managed to escape from the plantations and the mines, searching for freedom in the mountains and forests. Running away, temporarily or permanently, could be an individual or collective action. At times, it was part of a more concerted effort of rebellion. Those who managed to escape capture, were called *cimarrones* (wild, untamed) by the Spanish, from which the word 'Maroon' is derived.

For mutual support they banded together to form communities that went by a number of different names: Maroons, Palenques, Quilimbos. Maroon communities emerged as free and independent societies that forced colonial governments to sign treaties and pacts guaranteeing their freedom and autonomy. For planters, treaties with Maroon communities had two significant objectives: supporting the local militia to secure the return of runaways and supporting the planter class in putting down rebellions. In short, to become the planters' police.

In many locations, Maroon communities were able to develop a unique sense of identity and history, and become repositories of an African culture that was constantly under threat on the plantation. Today, descendants of some of the original Maroon communities live in Jamaica, Surinam, Cayenne, Colombia, Mexico, Texas, and the Bahamas. One of the most famous Maroon communities is the one in Jamaica. Its development started with the British takeover of the island in 1655, which provided an opportunity for enslaved Africans to retreat to the mountains. Over centuries their numbers were added to by runaways. Two Maroon Wars were fought with the British: 1725-39 and 1795-96. The second Maroon War led to the deportation of one branch of the Maroon community to Nova Scotia and thence to Sierra Leone.

An equally famous Maroon community was the one established by the great quilimbo leader, Zumbi, in the

Monument to the Quilimbo leader, Zumbi, Brazil.

mountains of Palmares in the Pernambuco region of Brazil. The quilimbo was divided into eleven fortified sites. Using guerrilla tactics and the deadly martial arts of capoeira, they defeated seven attacks by Portuguese/Brazilian military forces and by an invading Dutch army. The Palmares Republic, as it was called, managed to preserve its independence for nearly 100 years (1605-94). At its height, the republic supported a population of 20,000 free African from six different cultures. Zumbi is today a hero for Afro-Brazilians.

An alternative to marronage was conspiracy and rebellion. The Three Continents, One History Project website timeline demonstrates that from the first documented rebellion of Africans in the New World in 1519, there was never a period in the history of the Americas when rebellions and conspiracies were not a powerful feature of life.

Scholars have spent a lot of time trying to identify the conditions that have been conductive to the outbreak of rebellions: rising and falling expectations, unusual hardships and economic distress, the role of religion, and so on. From the Santidade movement of late 16th century Brazil to the Black Baptists of Jamaica's Christmas Rebellion in 1831-32, religion has provided rebels with leadership, organisation, ideologies and a community of feeling.

The significant influence of Sam 'Daddy' Sharpe in using his position as a preacher in the Native Baptist church to organise the general strike that started the Christmas rebellion is well known. The stated aim was to secure wages for their labour; and if wages were not paid, the rebels would take their freedom by force. The revolt spreads from St James to Hanover, Westmoreland and Manchester and involved some 20,000 enslaved Africans. In the parish of Manchester, the insurgency coincided with a local Muslim-inspired rebellion led by Mohammed Kaba.

In Brazil, the series of revolts that took pace in Bahia between 1807 and 1835 – 1807, 1809, 1814, 1816 1822, 1826, 1828, 1829, 1830, 1835 – reveal the importance of traditional African religions (Yoruba in this case) and of Islam. Between 1807 and 1816 the Islamic influence on Bahian rebellions was quite marked. The first revolt of 1807 was organised by two Muslims of Hausa descent – Balthazar and Antonio – the first a slave the second a free man. After a period of quiet there was the well-documented Revolt of Malês, as African Muslims in Bahia were known. Though short-lived, the rebellion was one of best organised in Brazil. The involvement of free and more well-off Africans would suggest that it cannot be treated as a typical slave revolt. Hundreds of Africans occupied the streets of the Bahian capital of San Salvador and engaged in fighting with the Brazilian military. The leaders of the rebellion were figures such as Shaykh Dandara, Shaykh Sanim, Malam Bubakar Ahuna, Malam Bilal Licutan, Imam Manuel Calafate, Silvestre Jose Antonio, Thomas, Dassala, and Nicobe. Conservative estimates suggests that over 500 people were put to death. Fearing a repetition, an attempt was made to forcibly convert Muslims to Catholicism.

In between the various Muslim inspired rebellions in Brazil, there were a number of rebellions – notably the Uruba revolt of 1826 - that were directly influenced by African traditional religions. On this occasion Africans ran away from their plantations and took refuge in a quilombo called Uruba, a traditional centre for the practice

Painting by Augustus Earle, 1824, depicting the deadly martial art of capoeira, developed during the sixteenth century by Angolan slaves in their struggles against the Portuguese, Brazilians and Dutch. To mask its intentions, capoeira was often presented as a dance or game.

Above: Toussaint L'Ouverture, architect of the Haitian Revolution. Saint-Remy, *Vie de Toussaint L'Ouverture*, 1850. British Library Board. All rights reserved.

Below: Revenge Taken by the Black Army for the cruelties practiced on them by the French! Engraving by J. Barlow in Marcus Rainsford (1805) *An Historical Account of the Black Empire of Haiti.*

of Cadomble (a combination of Yoruba orisha and Christian practices). From their base at Uruba, Africans began by raiding some of the surrounding villages before retreating back into the forest. Yoruba, and sometimes Ewe, spiritual and cultural beliefs were to play a significant role in the life of Afro-Brazilians. They became a unifying force in the struggle against slavery and the desire to define a space that was outside the disciplinary regime of slavery.

Sometimes rebellions deepened into Wars of Liberation. This situation obtained in Guyana in 1763, Grenada and St Lucia in 1795. Though these rebellions-cum-liberation wars eventually failed, this was not the case in Haiti (St Domingue) where the rebellion became a full-blooded revolution.

HAITIAN REVOLUTION

After the voodun ceremony in the Bois Caiman, the Haitian revolution kicked off with a massive slave revolt on 21st August in northern Haiti (Le Cap) led by Boukman, a houngan/priest of the Petwo Voodoo cult, and other key figures such as Jean-Francois, Biassou and Jeannot. Asserting their commitment to equality and the 'rights of man', these uprisings became a coordinated insurrection, as tens of thousands seized their estates and murdered their masters. Toussaint L'Ouverture soon joined the rebels with an army of 55,000.

The increasing radicalisation of the French Revolution – the beheading of the King and the declaration of a republic proclaiming the rights and liberties of 'men' – encouraged Britain to invade the island. Despite some initial successes, British forces were unable secure the support of Africans and 'mulattos' in the absence of any ability to promise freedom at the end of service as the Spanish forces had done after crossing the border from the Dominican Republic.

In the summer of 1793, three new French Commissioners reached the colony. Recognising that the only way to outmanoeuvre the invading British and Spanish armies and save Haiti for France, the Republican Commissioner, Leger-Felicité Sonthonax, proclaimed slave emancipation in the territory on 1st August 1793. A year later the National Convention in Paris went one step further by promulgating a general emancipation decree for all French territories. Toussaint now rallied to the French cause and drove the Spanish out of the island in 1794. Using the guerrilla tactics, Toussaint - then Governor of Haiti - proceeded to take on the British army and secured their capitulation in 1798 when General Maitland sued for safe passage out of the island having lost some 40,000 troops.

Events in Paris changed significantly after 1799, when Napoleon, the new French Head of State, issued a declaration to restore slavery in 1802. The die was cast when the French despatched an invasion force of 20,000 to engage Toussaint and his generals in a number of battles,. Acting on Napoleon's instructions to make promises that they would never keep, the head of the French invasion force, General Leclerc, seized Toussaint by deceit during a meeting, and deported him to France where he later died in prison in 1803. This subterfuge reignited the campaign after rebel leaders, including maroons, met to elect Dessalines as commander-in-chief. A further 10,000 French troops arrived. Under the new leadership of Rochambeau, the French forces made gains in early

1803. Heartened by the successful reimposition of slavery in Guadeloupe, Napoleon sent a further 15,000 troops. The fighting was extremely brutal. French troops committed many atrocities in their attempt to bring the island under control and restore slavery. African freedom-fighters responded likewise.

Under the ruthless leadership of Dessalines, the French were pushed back to Le Cap. French soldiers died in droves from the fighting and from yellow fever. With the realisation that a new outbreak of war in Europe would prevent Napoleon from sending further reinforcements to Saint Domingue to relieve the besieged and starving troops, Rochambeau begged for a ten-day truce to allow the evacuation of Le Cap. After thirteen years of freedom fighting, the independence of Saint Domingue was declared by Jean-Jacques Dessalines on January 1st 1804 using the name given to it by the original inhabitants: Haiti.

LESS FAMILIAR HEROES AND HEROINES
Queen Nzinga (Dona Ana de Souza)
Queen Nzinga Mbande was born into Kongoloese aristocracy around 1582. Nzinga was the name given to her because of the umbilical chord wrapped around her neck at birth. She lived at a time when the Portuguese had consolidated their power in the region to increase the volume of Africans taken. The first discussion of her is when she accompanied her brother, Ngola Ngola Mbande, at a peace conference with the Portuguese Governor Joao Correia de Sousa aimed at securing Portuguese withdrawal from the fortress they had built on Ndongo territory. The story is told that the Governor provided no chair for her to sit on during the negotiations, putting her at a diplomatic disadvantage. Refusing to sit on the floor, a position suitable only for inferiors, she proceeded to sit on the back of one of her retinue.

The Portuguese never honoured the treaty. On the death of her brother she assumed the position of regent to her nephew in 1624. With the death of the nephew – some say that she had him killed – she assumed sovereign power in Ndongo. War with the Portuguese forced Nzinga to abandon her capital. She regrouped, raised an army and took over the neighbouring Kingdom of Matamba in 1631. Her victories in battles which she personally led, led her to encourage her subjects to call her 'King' rather than 'Queen'.

She sought to make an alliance with the rival European nation of Netherlands which was challenging Portuguese hegemony in the region in order to recover Ndongo. Though she succeeded in defeating the Portuguese at Ngoleme in 1644, her capital, Kavanga, fell to the Portuguese in 1646. Dutch reinforcements helped to relieve the pressure. Further Portuguese victories led her to retreat to Matamba where she carried on the struggle until her death in 1663.

Kimpa Vita (Dona Beatriz)
Kimpa Vita (1682-1707) was an aristocrat and prophetess who lived in the Kingdom of Kongo at a time when the country was going through an irreversible period of turmoil caused by rapacious attempt by the Portuguese to capture and traffick in large numbers of her country men/women. Possessed by the spirit of St Anthony of

Above: General Jean Jaques Dessalines. He steered Haiti to independence, in 1804, after the imprisonment and death of Touissant.
Below: Queen Nzinga Mbande (1582-1663), Congolese aristocrat and Queen of Matamba who led a long campaign to expel the Portugese from her country.

THREE CONTINENTS, ONE HISTORY

Padua, a popular Catholic Saint and miracle worker, she began preaching in the capital, Mbanza Kongo (San Salvador), about the need for unity. To her popular supporters she claimed that Mbanza Kongo was Bethlehem; that Jesus, Mary and other Christian saints were really Kongolese; Christ and the saints were black; heaven was for Africans only; and that Africans should not listen to European missionaries. Though she was burned at the stake for heresy, her ideas – the Antonian movement – were adopted as a point of unification for the Kingdom. Today, her ideas are still circulate.

Tula and Bastiaan Karpata

1795 was a critical year in the life of Dutch colony of Curaçao. In Europe, Holland had become a vassal state of the French Republic and renamed the Batavian Republic after the King had fled to England. Enslaved Africans in Curaçao followed closely these developments, as well as the events unfolding in Haiti and nearby Venezuela where runaway Africans from Curaçao had participated in a significant rebellion in Coro aimed at bringing slavery to an end in Venezuela. Africans in Curaçao waited in expectation that the decree of the French National Convention of 1794 to abolish slavery in all French territories would apply equally to the colonies of the Batavian Republic. When the colonial government showed no sign of following suit, hoping perhaps that Britain would intervene and take over the colony to protect the slaving interest, Africans decided to take matters into their own hands. Four leaders of the struggle emerged: Tula, Bastiaan Karpata, Pedro Wakao and the military strategist Louis Mercier.

After weeks of preparation, the revolt commenced on the 17th August 1795 when Africans led by Tula told the owner of Kenepa plantation, Gaspar Lodewijk van Uytrecht, that they would no longer work for him. The rebels moved to the neighbouring plantation of Sint Kruis where they were joined by more rebels led by Karpata. Together they moved from plantation to plantation freeing more Africans to the refrain:

"We are here to win or die; We want our freedom".

Slave owners retreated to the capital, Willemstad, to plan their counter strategy leaving their plantations unprotected. An initial force sent to engage the rebels was defeated. At the behest of the strategist and commander Louis Mercier, the rebels began a guerrilla campaign of poisoning wells and stealing food. The Colonial Council regrouped and mobilised a force of armed horsemen and a 'korps vrije negers, mulatten' (a corps of freed Negroes and mulattoes). There followed a brutal and bloody onslaught in which the leaders of the revolution were executed at Ref. After seven weeks the revolt had come to an end. Today, Tula and Karpata are revered as fighters for human rights and independence.

Solitude

As elsewhere in the Caribbean, the 1790s were a critical period in the history of Guadeloupe. Slavery had been abolished in Guadeloupe in 1794 and the invading British army had been kicked out. The fragile freedom enjoyed

Below Left: Monument erected to commemorate the leaders of the Curacao slave revolution of August 1795 depicting Tula, Karpata and Mercier.
Below Right: Solitude: pregnant heroine and commander of Maroon forces, fighting French attempt to reimpose slavery in Guadeloupe, 1802.

by Africans was immediately threatened by Napoleon's determination to restore slavery in French territories. In 1802 Napoleon sent an invasion force under General Richepanse to Guadeloupe to retake the island. In the struggle that followed, the figure of Solitude enters the pages of Guadeloupean history. History has it that she was born around 1772 to an African mother who was raped aboard a slave ship across the Middle Passage. Her green eyes and colouring set her apart from other enslaved Africans. At the age of eight her mother fled the plantation. In her adolescence she vowed to fight against slavery by becoming a 'nègre marron' (freedom fighter). She took the name of Solitude. Though heavily pregnant in 1802, she assumed the position of commander of a band of nègres marrons at Dolé to assist the freedom struggle led by Ignace and Delgrès, and to ensure that her child would be born into a free Guadeloupe. Dolé was the scene of a key battle in the campaign. Solitude's heroic campaign against the well-armed forces of General Richepanse was defeated. She was captured and executed on the 29th November 1802. Before she died, slavery had been reimposed in Guadeloupe on May 20, 1802.

Josef Caridad Gonzalez

After fleeing the island of Curacao, Caridad Gonzalez, an African from Loango, settled in a palenque near the town of Coro in Venezuela. The Coro and Falcon region was an area to which runaway Africans from plantations in the Dutch islands of Curaçao and Bonaire had gravitated. After local Venezuelan planters sought to block the implementation of 1789 Black Code 'Carolino', enslaved Africans and maroons organised a rebellion which started in May 1795. There laid out their demands:

(1) Implementation of the 'French Law', i.e. establishment of a democratic republic along the lines of the French Revolution
(2) Freedom for enslaved Africans and the abolition of slavery
(3) Suppression of the taxes imposed on the indigenous peoples
(4) Elimination of the white aristocracy.

Though this rebellion was put down, it laid the foundation for the struggle for national independence that was soon to be pursued by Europeans like Simon Bolivar. Independence, however, came without the abolition of slavery which continued until 1850.

Coffy (Cuffee)

The Berbice rebellion in Guyana led by Coffy in 1763 was one that almost succeeded in taking over the whole Dutch colony. The rebellion started when enslaved Africans destroyed the Magdalenenburg plantation and killed the manager and carpenter, and burned down the owner's house. They then moved on to other plantations urging support for their cause. Very quickly, the rebels were organised as a fighting force by Coffy, who was a house-slave on a plantation that was also in revolt. His deputy was Akara. Other leaders who emerged were Atta and Accabre, Cossala and and Goussari. As the rebels marched towards the capital, numbers increased. The rebels set up headquarters at Fort Nassau. From here Coffy wrote to the Dutch governor claiming the whole territory and signing the letter, 'Governor of Berbice'. His opening gambit was to divide the colony with the northern part ruled by whites and the south by Africans. A split in the ranks of the rebels enabled the new Dutch forces assembled to take advantage and crush the rebellion.

Gaspar Yanga

During early period of Spanish rule in New Spain (Mexico), enslaved Africans led by Gaspar Yanga – said to have come from Gabon - revolted on the lowland sugar plantations around the coastal town of Veracruz in 1570. They fled to the nearby mountains which had become the home to a number of independent maroon communities. In an inaccessible part of the mountain Yanga built a palenque or free maroon community of 500 people. The palenque survived by raiding Spanish caravans bound for Veracruz.

The growth of the community over the next thirty years led the Spanish authorities to the decision that Yanga had to be crushed. A military force of 550 well-armed men was despatched from the city of Puebla in 1609 to destroy the palenque. . On hearing of the expedition, Yanga, then an old man, delegated military strategy to an Angolan, Francisco de la Matosa. The latter proceeded to organise the fighters, arming them with a few old conquistador muskets, rocks, machetes and bows and arrows. Using guerrilla tactics, de la Matosa beat back the first foray by the Spanish army. Not wishing to retreat further into the mountains, Yanga proposed a peace treaty the substance of which was the idea of a homeland in which the palenque would govern itself on domestic matters while paying taxes to the government and swearing loyalty to the Spanish Crown in times of foreign invasion. The stumbling block to any agreement was what to do with the volume of runaway Africans who would naturally continue to seek refuge in this free palenque. Yanga offered to return any new runaways who sought asylum in the territory administered by him after 1608. A further skirmish ensued with heavy losses on both sides. Yanga's forces retreated further into the mountains. The prospect of pursing the freed Africans further into the mountains, and being picked off by guerrilla tactics, led the Spanish to agree to the terms set out by Yanga under which the palenque would be allowed to return to its arable land on Mount Totutla. In the final agreement, the Viceroy agreed to move the Yangans to better farmland in the lowlands. The town of Yanga, formerly knows as San Lorenzo de los Negros, survives to this day, and has a population of 20,000. Since the work done by Riva Palacio to excavate the history of the palenque, Yanga has become a Mexcian national hero. A statue was put up in the town; and since 1986, there has been an annual August 'Festival of Negritude' to celebrate the town's founder.

Cecile Fatiman

Cécile Fatiman (Creole: Sesil Fatima) was a mambo (female voodun priest) and leader of the voodun ceremonies that took place in the Caiman Forest on 14 August, 1791. She invoked the vodou spirit of Ezili Danto. The

Gaspar Yanga: The leader of a maroon community in Mexico who forced Spanish authorities to recognise the autonomy of his palenque or free maroon community. Photo by John Todd Jr.

ceremony sparked the early stages of the Haitian Revolution and still resonates strongly among Haitians to this day. Fatiman, a mulatto, was married to Louis Michel Pierrot, one of the leaders of the battle of Vertieres which Jean-Jacques Dessalines commanded. Fatiman lived to the ripe old age of 112.

Carlota

The province of Matanzas was the scene of many confrontations between Africans and the Cuban slave regime, particularly during the 1840s. The massive expansion of sugar production in the island had sucked in large numbers of Africans who had come from particular regions like Nigeria, particularly after the fall of the Oyo Confederacy in 1836. Carlota was a *lukumi* or Yoruba woman. Together with two fellow lukumi, Evaristo and Fermina, she took up a machete and led a campaign which started at the Triumvirato ingenio or estate in Matanzas in 1843 to encourage her fellow Africans to rise up and overthrow the yoke of enslavement. By means of talking drums, the rebels sought to co-ordinate their actions to free Africans on other ingenios. A few days after the rebellion began, the *Vandalia*, a U.S. navy corvette, entered Havana harbour and offered assistance to the planters. This support spurred the Spanish authorities and slave-owning oligarchy to unleash a reign of terror on enslaved Africans that was infamous for its cruelty. Carlota was captured in early 1844, and her body was tied two horses pulling in opposite directions and ripped apart. In Cuban history, 1844 has become known as the 'year of the lashes'.

6

The expression of Africa through Jamaican and Black British Music

Sophia 'Ankhobia' Carvalho

The Djembe is the drum of the Mandinka people, and its origins dates back to the Mali Empire of the 12th century. Courtesy Birmingham Museums & Art Gallery.

RETENTION AND PRESERVATION

African musical heritage is a major influence in contemporary Black diasporic culture. It reflects the movement of people and cultures across three continents. The journey began with the Trans Atlantic trade in Africans from central and west Africa to the Caribbean. As Caribbean people migrated they took their musical heritage with them, for example to the UK and America. Africans in the diaspora have, over five centuries of struggle, carved out the unique neo-African sounds of calypso, soca, zouk, pop, reggae, dancehall, Cuban son, Puerto Rico salsa, rock'n'roll, compas, merengue, American blues, jazz, gospel, soul, grime, hip hop, garage, drum'n'bass, r'n'b and so much more. These styles have drawn heavily from the African musical landscape and have in turn affected the development of contemporary African music, i.e. African dancehall and hip hop.

In this chapter I will explore the legacy of west and central African music in the development of Jamaican and Black British music. The discussion does not tell the whole story of African musical migration across three continents, but rather explores particular themes and traditions across time and space. Thus I shall ask the key question: How do these neo-African music genres express Africa? How does Africa survive in the music and, if not, then why?

AFRICAN MUSIC

Although a diverse continent, across Africa one can find commonalities amongst the thousands of cultures that exist. The history of ancient African music dates as far back as ancient Egypt, which is very important in understanding the interconnectedness between African music styles, despite different geographical locations. Take for instance the Nigerian instrument the double reed pipe found amongst the Hausa people, this was also found in the tomb of the boy king Tutankhamen. Or the sansel in Ethiopia, in ancient Egypt they called it the sistrum. Ancient Egypt was important as a source of musical instruments, diatonic scales (doh, reh, me, fah, so, la, te, do), the source of harmonic theory, and musical academies. Given the commonalities that exist within African music, it can be categorized into three distinct groups: firstly, the classical music tradition which was played in the royal courts; secondly, traditional music; and finally, the popular sounds of today i.e. soukous, hi-life, kwaito, nu-Afro, highlife, ju ju, mbalax and so on.

CHARACTERISTICS OF AFRICAN MUSIC

Amidst the diversity of musical styles, African music has certain distinctive traits. One is the use of repetitive sounds, the simultaneous combination of several distinct musical parts. There is also the importance of rhythm and dominance of percussion. The African concept of music also involves the use of cross rhythms, that is many rhythms playing together (polyrhythms) creating their own rhythm. These instruments interlock to create complicated patterns, which are interwoven with each other to create a harmonious sound.

West African music is characterised by a strong beat that can also be played by the feet or body percussion of the dancers. Often emphasis in rhythm will change so that the usually unstressed 'weak' beat becomes the strong beat (syncopation). African music has a conversational quality often called 'call-and-response', which usually alternates between a soloist, and a chorus giving the lead singer more freedom to improvise. Instruments can also emulate call and response techniques. Then there is cellular structure; i.e., pieces built on repetition and variation on a short musical cell. Some improvisers can hide the melody in their complicated improvisations. African music also involves a lot of changes in pitch and tone so musicians and especially singers, perform with little regard to scales or pitch. They use the entire spectrum of notes, and rarely jump cleanly from one note to another giving the singers freedom to produce a wide variety of sounds.

INSTRUMENTS

Africa has a wide variety of musical instruments. These include:
Percussion: the xylophone (marimba), finger bell cow bells, the calabash, clap-sticks, bells, rattles, slit gongs, struck gourds and clay pots, stamping tubes. Other percussion instruments from Africa are the gonkogui, a traditional double bell which is held in the hand whilst being struck with a stick. The yenca rattle is a gourd containing seeds that make the sound. The toke or banana bell is played by striking it with a metal rod whilst it is laid across the palm of the hand.
Drums: includine the djembe drum which dates back to the twelfth century Mali Empire of West Africa, the sakara, a hand-held drum from Nigeria, and talking drums.
Stringed: musical bow, lute, lyre, harp, and zither, kora, and violins.
Wind: horns, trumpets, flutes, whistles and pan-pipes, oboe, ivory trumpet, and the double clarinet.

SOCIAL FUNCTIONS OF AFRICAN MUSIC

The 'purpose' of African music is not to produce music for its own sake or because it sounds pleasing to hear, but for a function or an event. There is no sound that cannot be used in African music and anything that can be blown, struck, shaken or rubbed is an instrument. Throughout all African societies music plays an integral role

Two jallis (griots) from Soolimana and Kooranko (Sierra Leone) with their musical instruments, early 1820s. Source: Alexander Gordon Laing, *Travels in the Timannee, Kooranko, and Soolima countries in Western Africa* (London, 1825).

> Praise poetry **Oriki** is a specialized skill and takes time to learn, memorize and be able to chant the oriki of individuals and families. This is a profession found generally amongst women and older people.

> 'A **griot** who dies, it is a library which burns'

Susu griot with lute, Conakry, Guinea c.1910. Collection of Shlomo Pestcoe, courtesy of www.shlomomusic.com

in the society and is used for various reasons such as: to celebrate life, to praise the creator, to accompany work, to prepare for war, for lullabies, to mourn the loss of a loved one, or even to sing someone's praises or perhaps critique a person's character. Music can also be used to engage ancestral spirits to aid healing. Perhaps the most important element of African music is the notion of community as expressed in the polyrhythmic nature of African music. It is the community, and not necessarily the individual, that creates the sound.

ORAL TRADITIONS

In traditional west African societies there was no separation between man and God, or man and his environment. Music therefore formed an important aspect of African philosophy. Music, singing and dance have always been central to Yoruba religion. For example, in a ceremony, music and dance are used to connect the physical world to the supernatural world of the gods (*orisha*) and ancestors (*egun*). Oriki (songs and praise poems to the orisha) would be sung to send the practitioners into trance opening a pathway for the orishas' divine energy (*ashe*) to enter. Various instruments are used, for example, the drum which helps to shape the ceremony and summon the orisha with their special rhythmic signatures, and dance, using sacred invocations.

Praise poems are a major part of west African culture and are closely linked and based on the African concept of the power of the word. The Yoruba's also use 'oriki' for the purpose of inspiration as an attribution to a person. They form an important part of Yoruba oral traditions. 'In Yoruba customs, people who have distinguished themselves in some way are acknowledged not just by name but also according to a description of their achievements and family lineage, which are expressed in their oriki.

MUSIC AS HISTORY

Some west African cultures have a stratum of society whose sole function is to act as cultural repositories, passing on ancestral 'folk' memories and teachings. These professional persons or families responsible for this task are called griots. Only the griot can recite the royal epics, the genealogies, the great battles, great families and great heroes. In a way they possess the history of their society. A griot is equivalent to a historian and journalist and more. He also writes and performs praise poetry. Because most of the information that is memorised is secret and specific to his society, most of it exists as a system of codified songs, which can only be fully understood if the listener also understands the language of the code.

Although, in some societies, female griots do exist the role is usually male and is passed within families, for example, from father to son, or uncle to nephew. Griots are expert musicians instrumentally and vocally, so no ceremony is complete without one being present.

THE NEW WORLD AND THE DEVELOPMENT OF AFRICAN MUSIC

The removal of millions of Africans from their homeland was a traumatic experience which ultimately created newer and more diverse ways of expressing African music in the new world of Jamaica. The majority of enslaved

Africans brought to Jamaica came from west African groups – mainly the Akan people of Ghana between Nigeria and the Ivory Coast, and from the Congolese-Angolan people of central Africa. For example in the seventeenth century the Ashanti-Fanti groups of the Gold Coast comprised 70 percent of enslaved Africans imported by the British compared to the central African Yoruba-Ibo groups who were imported in smaller numbers. Once they reached the Caribbean they were forbidden in many cases to practice their culture so they had to find new ways to try and preserve it and pass it on. In Jamaica enslaved Africans would try and continue their African traditions in an attempt to maintain links with their homelands, as they tried to survive in a cruel new world.

THE NEW WORLD – PLANTATION WORKSONGS

Just as in Africa where music accompanied all aspects of communal activity, so did it on the plantations of the Caribbean. It could be said that the first 'new' music created by Africans on Jamaican soil was plantation worksongs or 'digging songs'. Worksongs were used to coordinate slave labour in the field. It was the only means of communication that Africans were allowed whilst working. The music was also therapeutic in that it provided an outlet for pain, offering hope and comfort, and often relaying important messages. Worksongs retained many African musical traditions, for example, call and response. On the plantations a lead singer would sing a line by himself and fellow slaves would respond in chorus creating a communal activity. Beyond the cane-field, Africans also engaged in singing for recreational purposes. Visitors to plantations noted that the singing would begin around six o'clock in the evening and last until two in the morning, without a pause.

AFRICAN INSTRUMENTS IN JAMAICA

Africans would try to replicate the instruments from their native lands. This was done by using the natural resources found in Jamaica (calabash, conch, bamboo, etc.). From this came drums which could be shaken, rubbed or plucked and string instruments (like lutes and harps) to reproduce sounds. Soon music on the plantation provided the same social function as music in Africa. The music also had a political purpose in that drums would be used to send messages from one plantation to another, for example, to inform Africans on other plantations that a revolt was about to take place.

Music also served as a means to demonstrate power. For example, in west and central Africa, horn and drum music often expressed the power of the institution or state. In 1684 and 1694, travellers to the Gold Coast town of Gross Friedrichsberg, Johan Nieman and Otto Friedrich von der Groeben, had observed the elite horn and drum ensembles within Gold Coast societies, which played only for major political leaders. Because these musicians were deemed priceless, when captured during war, these royal court musicians could not be sold or traded by their new owners. It is unlikely that court musicians were sold into Jamaican slavery; they would have been rescued or ransomed by their own people or kept as a prize by their captors. The majority of enslaved Africans had come from regions which had musical traditions connected in some way to state displays of power. However it is said that the practice was strongest and most developed in the Gold Coast, and well known to

Above: Jalikebba Kuyateh, master of the Kora. Courtesy Jalikebba Kuyateh.
Below: Ashanti Yam Ceremony, ca. 1817. Source: Thomas E. Bowdich, *Mission from Cape Coast Castle to Ashantee* (London, 1819), showing procession involving the king and his officials, representatives from several European nations, musicians playing an assortment of instruments, and onlookers to mark the first day of the yam festival.

> Jamaican folk groups use a variety of instruments during worship, rituals and healing etc. These include:
>
> **Dinki Mini** (Benta, Bamboo and Gourd)
> **Jonkunoo** (Snare type Drum, Shakas, Rattler, Horn, Goombeh)
> **Kumina** (Kbandu Drum, Playing Cyas Drum, Grater)
> **Maroon** (Goombay Drums, 'kete Drum, Bench Drum, Cwat, Abeng/Conch)
> **Rastafari** (Repeater drum, Funde, Bass)
> **Revival** (Rattler Drum, Tenor Drum)
> **Ettu and Nago** (empty kerosene container struck with a nail and a double-headed drum).
> **Goombeh** (goombeh drum, which is a square frame drum with a goatskin head)

African ivory wind horn, similar to abeng horn used by Maroons in Jamaica. Courtesy Birmingham Museums & Art Gallery.

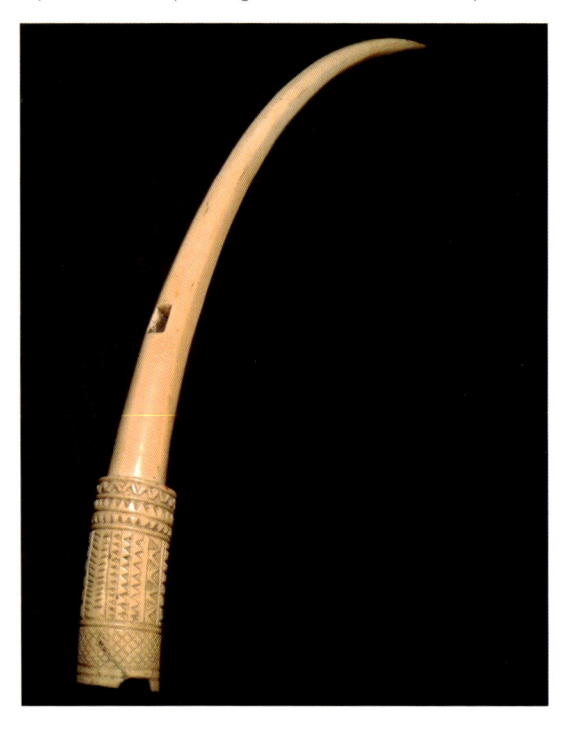

planters, missionaries, and traders.

In the new and hostile environment of the Caribbean, the Koromantis (a term used by Jamaica planters to refer to Africans purchased from Fort Cormantin in Ghana) recreated instruments and ensembles like those in their mother country. This was done to show their power both to their peers and to the planters. In the late seventeenth century there was a high rate of rebellions in Jamaica which was attributed in part to the music and also because many of the Koromantis came from strong military backgrounds. This music was so powerful that it frightened Jamaican planters and was 'prohibited by the Customs of the Island.' In Jamaica, enslaved Africans used court and folk music as a form of direct resistance to counter the planter's suppression of their culture and traditions and the threat posed to their existence. It has been reported that right up to the 1920s, an eight-stringed harp was still being used in Jamaica.

After the Koromanti-led revolts of the 1670s and 1680s, Africans from the Bight of Benin were brought into Jamaica. They accounted for about 30 percent of the Africans imported into Jamaica in the 1680-90s. Planters also turned to Angola (Kongo, Angola, Loango) in the same period. Because these people spoke Bantu languages and shared many cultural traits, it was easier to recreate their culture and traditions in Jamaicans. From about 1680 to 1700, Angolans constituted 40 percent of enslaved Africans brought into Jamaica. However just like Koromantis the planters found them hard to control as they would often run away. Thus planters would return to purchasing Koromantis and related Gold Coast groups.

JAMAICAN FOLK MUSIC

From the plantation experiences of these various African groups evolved the folk traditions of Jamaica which enabled the enslaved to retain a sense of identity. Thus slavery created the space for people to speak musically about political and social experiences and also, through ritual, to hold onto African culture.

Folk forms are comprised of three groups: songs for work and entertainment, religious worship and dance music. Jamaicans held onto their African traditions through folk forms like ettu, nago, tambo, goombeh, kumina, maroon, dinki mini, burru and pocomania music.

It is because of Jamaican folk music that the musical sounds dominating the Jamaican musical landscape can be more identified with African vocal sounds, dance styles, and rhythms. This does not however dismiss the European (British, Celtic, Scottish, Irish and Welsh) elements of harmony, melody and instrumental compositions.

As with its predecessors ska and rock steady, reggae would merge musical traditions and cultural/spiritual facets from Africa: the traditional shuffle, mento, American rhythm 'n' blues, soul, African-Protestant revivalist music and other Caribbean rhythms like calypso, merengue, and rumba.

Rastafarian leaders, such as Count Ossie and Leonard Howell, in their yearning to retain their links with ancient Africa, learnt the ancient drumming tradition of burru. The Burru people belonged to the old Kongo kingdom. It is from the African burru musicians that we get the akete drum rhythm in reggae music today. For example the famous song 'Pass The Cuchie', sang by the Mighty Diamonds, which provided a 1980s hit (Pass the

Dutchie) for Birmingham reggae band Musical Youth, has been traced back to the burru song 'Pass the Pipe'. As the Rasta faith developed amongst new practitioners kumina music was fused with burru drums (the bass, fundeh and repeater) and called nyabinghi music. Nyabinghi drumming and philosophy played a very important role in the development of reggae music.

Reggae provides social, spiritual and political commentary on an array of issues. Reggae musicians, like their griot ancestors, used music to protest against the injustices of colonialism and provide commentary about daily life. The most famous reggae griot of all is Bob Marley. As a result of the lessons that he had with Alvin 'Francesco' Patterson, he introduced nyabinghi chants and drumming into his music. He often sang about the brutality and poverty he witnessed, and also used the music to spread the message of Black redemption through reclaiming African heritage. Rastafarians also use the music in the same manner as the Koromantis from Ghana to show their power in an oppressive society. Rastafarian musicians will often comment that reggae music is the 'Kings' music and that they are merely his (Haile Selassie's) messengers.

Another important African dynamic in the formation of reggae music is the role of African spiritual traditions. It is alleged that the primary creator for the reggae sound was Lee Scratch Perry. He is reported to have said that he was trying to recreate the energy and spirit of the Pocomanian revivalist church music. Other influences are the African call and response patterns from African-derived work and grave songs 'part singing, antiphonal call-response chanting, and the repetition of single short musical phrases', the use of percussion, drummers playing polyrhythmic, using the voice or horns to recreate sliding pitches and untempered scale tones.

> 'An accomplished hand drummer, (Franseeco) had worked with a number of Jamaica's calypso groups. The Burru style of drumming he played was an African rhythm of liberation welcoming the return of released prisoners of war; it had been co-opted into Rastafari's Nyabinghi rhythms. And it was this blend of devotion and rebellious fervour that formed the basis of Nesta's (Bob Marley) understanding of rhythm.'
>
> **Adrain Boot and Chris Salewicz**
> *Bob Marley: Songs of Freedom*

JAMAICAN MUSIC FAMILY TREE

African Music
↓
Plantation Worksongs
↓
Folk Music — Ettu, Nago, Tambo, Goombeh, Kumina, Maroon, Dinki mini, Burru

- American Jazz & RnB → Jamaican Jazz & RnB
- Mento → Mento Jazz → Trinidadian Calypso
- Folk Music → Mento
- Folk Music → Kumina Burru (Kumina, Pocomania, Burru Revivalism) → Nyahbinghi

Popular Music: Ska; Rock Steady; Rub A Dub/Lovers Rock; Reggae; Dub; Deejay/Dancehall.

> 'I am one of the architects of hip hop culture along with other comrades brother Kool DJ Herc who we call the father, myself and the Grandmaster Flash and then all the other pioneers who came after us … hip hop has its roots in funk or what James brown, Sly & The Family Stone and George Clinton from Parliament Funkadelic gave, and it also has its roots in reggae or ragga starting with I-Roy, U-Roy and Who-Roy and myself Africa Bambaataa, Grandmaster Flash, Kool DJ Herc all are from Westindian backgrounds. Kool DJ Herc is Jamaican, myself Jamaica and Barbados and Grandmaster Flash, Barbados…and it all goes back to Africa…I was influenced in Calypso by the Mighty Sparrow, Kitchener, Calypso Rose, The Mighty Shadow um so many groups and then in reggae you had I-Roy, U-Roy, Who-Roy, Trinity um Yelllowman was one of the first biggest stars that started traveling out, in hop hop you couldn't get a day of not playing a song without playing Yellowman. It was due to the Zulu Nation that we never gave up our roots and let everyone know in hip hop here is the reggae we playing the reggae, we played the soca, we played our salsa, our Latino roots because that Latino is also us …so we just kept all that alive to let everyone know that this is culture…'
>
> **Africa Bambaataa – The Godfather of Hip-hop (interview with author).**

Reggae vocals use a more irregular and natural tone. Like African music it does not follow a specific pattern of notes, so singers can express a wider variety of emotions.

Reggae's influence can be felt worldwide, whether it is in drum 'n' bass, hip hop, African dancehall, African reggae, rave and dance culture – reggae is there.

CARIBBEAN MIGRATION AND THE EVOLUTION OF JAMAICAN MUSIC

> "Urban music in the west is divorced from its spiritual
> context, because it operates more on a business level i.e. studios, tv,
> tours etc. It's the business aspect of the music that has removed
> the whole spiritualism out of the music. But it is still the
> same people (Black people) playing the music."
>
> Jazz percussionist and curator, Ola Lekan Babalola

Between 1955 and 1962 a quarter of a million people migrated from the Caribbean to the UK, over half of whom came from Jamaica. In a second wave of migration 350,000 African Caribbeans moved to the USA in search of work. As Jamaican migrants travelled to yet another new world, like their African ancestors, they would take with them their musical heritage. Once again Jamaican music would undergo several reincarnations as it adapted to a new environment. In the USA the children of Caribbean migrants in New York, such as Barbadian Grandmaster Flash, Africa Bambataa, DJ Kool Herc and Krs One, laid the foundation for hip-hop music. They drew heavily from the sound system and deejay culture of Jamaica and took on the role of African griots, speaking about all aspects of their environment.

On the other side of the Atlantic, the children of the Windrush generation, like their Caribbean cousins in America, would continue to draw on their Jamaican heritage, often borrowing from their African-American cousins to create the innovative sounds of garage, drum 'n' bass and lovers rock, whilst also producing some great soul, reggae and r'n'b artists/groups. In the late 1980s dancehall was used as the template for the UK rave scene, which in turn formed the template for the present dance and club scene. In the 1990s dancehall reggae was speeded up and remixed by Black youths living in the UK. They added reggae, African drums and riffs to hardcore rave music to create jungle music. UK artists have redefined what it is to be Jamaican within a Black British context. Artists who have emerged from this scene are Ms Dynamite, So Solid Crew, Big Brovas, Dizzee Rascal, The Anthill Mob and The Heartless Crew. All of these groups and individuals have incorporated elements of Jamaican culture into their music, drawing heavily on the legacy of the griot and some characteristics of African music. But it is not just the dancehall that has been a carrier of Jamaican culture; the church has also been an incubation for Jamaican and African retentions in Black British culture. Within Britain, Black churches which have more of an African orientation in their method of worship are the Baptist, Spiritual Baptists, and Pentecostal churches which tend to feature more African retentions in their services. Although participants would probably not equate any aspect of their Saturday or Sunday morning services with African modes of worship, the evidence speaks for itself: going into trance, speaking in tongues, the way in which the music is played and sung, and how the congregation interact with the music and the delivery of the service by the minister.

MARKET FORCES

In a capitalist society in which music is compartmentalized so that it can be packaged and sold, the essence of one's cultural expression can be lost. This is further compounded by dominant British music culture which is pop music that is primarily produced for domestic consumption. The struggle for Black British music, created against the backdrop of hostility, racism and, in some cases poverty, then becomes the challenge to recreate Black music to gain mainstream acceptance. This has often meant that Black artists have had to water down their music (don't sound too Black) in an attempt to be successful and reach audiences outside of Black culture. This watering down affect naturally lessens the presence of Jamaican culture and therefore African retentions in Black British music as it cannot be fully expressed. Black artists have been forced to reproduce Black pop or reggae with a European/British sound. This has a knock on effect in that Black audiences no longer see the music as true to its roots or culture i.e. 'inauthentic'. The music is also seen as 'not representing' or 'keeping it real' and therefore Black audiences turn to the music of Jamaica and African Americans or some underground Black British artists, who are seen as staying more in touch with the heartbeat of Black musical expression and therefore 'true to the game'. The British music industry cannot control what comes out of America but they can control what is exported from the UK. This has meant that they can export Black culture without Black people. Practically, this has sometimes meant that white British artists can successfully appropriate Black sounds and culture, i.e. UB40 is the biggest reggae band in the world, while other white artists such as Amy Winehouse, Mike Skinner, Joss Stone and Lilly Allen benefit from Black culture in a way that Black British artists do not and cannot. There is clearly a market for Black music within the UK, stemming from the success of American r'n'b and hip hop artists.

Black artists also face another struggle because any attempts to reproduce Jamaican or African American sounds are viewed as poor imitations 'copy cat music'; although the genres, irrespective of geographical location, come from the same musical tree and legacy – Africa. Furthermore Black music genres have always interchanged and borrowed from each other, putting their own unique spin on the sound that is then produced. Black British artists who attempt to do this can sometimes miss out the vibe and feeling that is generally associated with Black music.

THE CHATTELISATION OF BLACK CULTURE

In today's market, radical music is seen as a threat to the social order with the potential to create revolutionary change. The 'powers that be' need music that is non-revolutionary, music with form but no content, music that

> '…the Bristol scene for example, comes out of sound systems operating in the late seventies/early eighties, and out of that melting pot comes Portishead, Tricky, Finlay Quaye, Massive Attack, the Trip-Hop direction. Again it's all about sound system style; rapping, sampling, putting beats and rhythms together, and even the name that it now goes under; drum and bass, that's what they used to put on the B sides of Jamaican records during the early seventies, before it was called dub. So it's all inspired by Jamaican culture and it is a new thing, and it's gone far. In America now they call it 'electronica', which is drum and bass, which is reggae derived…'
>
> **An Interview with Steve Barrow, by Mark Downie.**

does not challenge the status quo and can be reproduced for mass consumption. Thus the market is more geared towards music that can be easily discarded and that does not have longevity. The sounds that get the most airplay are the 'love' and 'light hearted' songs that are a-political in content. Black diasporic music has always had a radical edge. In a capitalist music market, it is difficult for Black British artists to survive unless they water down not only their sound but also their message. Even those Black artists who follow mainstream definitions of black music (i.e. r'n'b singers like Jamelia and Beverley Knight) still have difficulty getting a foothold in the pop market. It would seem that in the UK that there is a 'chattellisation' of Black culture; Black music that is not allowed the freedom to fully express itself in the mainstream. Just as African music was forced to readapt in order to survive in Jamaica, by practicing their culture 'underground', or merging it with European sounds and religious expression etc, then it can be said that this 'chattellisation' is what is happening to Black music in the UK today. Some would say it has been happening since the late '70s and early '80s.

As the Black population in Britain is not increasing, the buying public remains small, with the result that the reproduction of Caribbean and African culture becomes difficult. In Jamaica the national music is reggae. It has massive support at home and abroad, for example, it accounts for 60 percent of the Caribbean music market and is constantly influenced by other diasporic sounds within the Caribbean. In America there are 50 million Black people, so an array of genres can survive even if the mainstream market is trying to create a 'synthetic version of so-called Black culture' that can be mass reproduced. Many Black British artists have now taken their music to the Caribbean or African-American markets.

However there is hope in that the influx of large numbers of illegal immigrants from across the Caribbean, in particular Jamaica, will lead to a revival of Black culture in the UK. These new immigrants, including Africans, also provide a space for Black British people to tap into their Caribbean and African heritage and culture and produce sounds that represent them regardless of the mainstream market. This can also provide underground artists the opportunity to continue to create music with form and content with the same characteristics, social function and dynamics as African music.

BIRMINGHAM
AND THE EUROPEAN SLAVE TRADE

7

Birmingham's Manufacturing Industries

Dr Clive Harris

Made in Birmingham, manillas exported to West Africa as a form of currency to be exchanged for Africans.

The intimate relationship between the development of Birmingham as a premier manufacturing city and the European trafficking in Africans is one that is only gradually being told. To some extent this is a reflection of the 'last day' focus of scholars who are more comfortable celebrating what they see as the 'moral transformation' of British society between 1787 and 1807 – which allegedly led to the suppression of the slave trade in 1807 and eventual abolition of slavery in 1838 – than in writing about the moral turpitude of the previous 225 years when Britain took a very active part in promoting and profiting from the trafficking in Africans. A second reason for the lack of focus on Birmingham is bound up with the fact that it has been far easier to tell the history of the ports like London, Bristol, Liverpool and Lancaster from which slaving ships could be seen visibly departing on a daily basis. Few people saw what was inside the holds of the ships as they departed from British waters bound for Africa. It is the valuable cargo that they carried that linked towns like Birmingham to Africa and to the Caribbean. A third reason for the lack of focus on Birmingham's connection with the trafficking derives from the selective telling of the city's abolitionist story which erases the murky past of a number of men who composed the Lunar Society – a group of 'men of letters' who, between 1765 and 1813, met on a monthly basis to examine how science and technology could be applied to fields such as manufacturing, transport, mining, and medicine. In a year when black abolitionists like Olaudah Equiano have been in the news, much has been made of the fact that this vanguard of the Industrial Revolution received Olaudah Equiano and sponsored his 'Narratives' when he visited the city in 1790. The irony is that, while bestriding the city intellectual landscape and harbouring abolitionist tendencies – 'gradual' abolition, that is – members of the Lunar Society such as Samuel Galton Jr, James Watt and Matthew Boulton were also actively engaged in propping up the trafficking in Africans and the system of enslavement that developed in the Caribbean.

From the moment that the trafficking in Africans was opened up by removing the monopoly exercised by the Royal African Company of Merchant Adventurers in 1698, and the United Kingdom acquired the Spanish asiento – the contract to transport Africans to the Spanish American territories – Birmingham grew dramatically.

Its close links with the emergent port of Bristol via the Severn River and its internal port of Bewdley, and proximity to local raw materials, gave it a competitive edge in supplying the various goods that merchants required for the 'African trade': guns, fetters, shackles, chains, brassware, and so on.

THE GUN INDUSTRY

From an early period in the trafficking in Africans, guns held their indispensable place in the cargo of the slaving ship. It was not, however, until the first order for flintlock muskets was placed in 1698 that Birmingham's gun industry began the long relationship with Africa that remained significant well into the 1880s. From an early period, Birmingham's 'African trade' was dominated by two Quaker gun merchants, Farmer & Galton (later Galton & Son). The partnership acted as organisers and controllers of hundreds of small specialist craftsmen scattered throughout Birmingham and the Black Country towns of Wednesbury, Darlaston and West Bromwich who made the constitutive components: locks, barrels, furniture, stocks, and so on. The firm's chief rivals in the city included companies such as Thomas Hadley and Joshua Adams; Benjamin Willets; Hyde & Lawson; Barker & Harris; Jordan & Oughton.

The output of these companies was a vast array of guns of varied quality. Not all were of the cheap, unproved quality that were derisively known in the trade as Park Palings or simply Gas Pipes. Some guns were well-finished and proved. The names of these 'Brummagem ware' quite often revealed the area of the West African coast where they were destined to be used (Bonny guns, Barbary guns, Angola guns, Windward muskets); the non-British merchants who had placed orders (Long and Short Danes, Spanish guns, Dutch guns); as well as the more specialist niche markets that were being supplied (Buccaneer guns, Swivel blunderbuss). The latter gun, because it emitted small shots over a wide area, was earmarked for use on slaving ships, where they would be kept permanently trained on the holds and exercise areas where Africans were assembled, to deter and put down insurrections. In addition to guns, Birmingham companies like Galton & Son supplied what became known in the trade as pacotille or ships stores. These included a varied collection of weapons such as pistols, cutlasses, knives and sheaths, which a small crew would need to overcome insurrections by several hundred Africans. Companies like Farmer & Galton represented a one-stop shop for a successful slaving journey.

At the beginning of the eighteenth century the Birmingham gun industry was fairly spread out within the town though with a concentration in the Digbeth area. By the middle of the eighteenth century, there was a

Above: Swivel blunderbuss.
Below: Map of Birmingham, 1731 (detail). Courtesy of Birmingham Archives & Heritage.

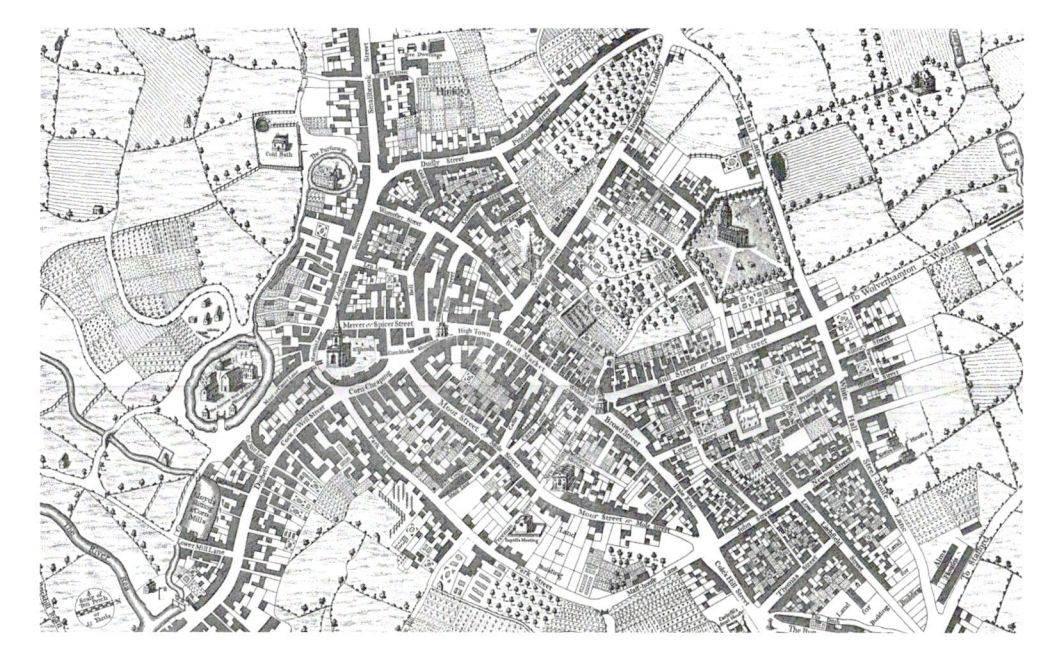

> Birmingham, May 18, 1789.
>
> WE are desired by several Gentlemen to request the Attendance of the Inhabitants of the Town of Birmingham, at the Public Office, in Dale-End, To-morrow, the 19th instant, at Eleven o'Clock in the Forenoon, to take into Consideration a Petition to Parliament, that the African Slave Trade (which is greatly and extensively Beneficial to this Town and Neighbourhood) may not be abolished, but undergo such Regulations only as are conducive to Humanity.
>
> JAMES PICKARD, THOMAS GREEN, } CONSTABLES.

Above: Petition by Birmingham manufacturers against the abolition of the slave trade, 1789. Courtesy of Birmingham Archives & Heritage.

Below: Trade card advertising plantation tools.

gradual shift towards the St Mary's area, the area bounded by Steelhouse Lane, and roughly coterminous with the Children's Hospital. By the middle of the eighteenth century, Birmingham had become the gun capital of the country, if not of Europe. If we assume that the number of guns carried by each slaving ship varied between 500 and 1,000, and that in 1771 nearly 200 slaving ships left the four main English slaving ports of Liverpool, Bristol, London and Lancaster, then we are talking here about 100,000 to 200,000 guns a year. In West Africa these guns were used to foment the internecine warfare between African societies. Birmingham armed the slave trade. The success of this arming of the trade ensured that there were few downturns in the Birmingham economy when skilled workers would have had to be laid off as invariably happened when companies were reliant on Ordnance contracts that fluctuated with the various wars fought between European nations.

In the 1750s the order books of companies like Farmer & Galton were bursting at the seams. In 1754 alone the company produced 12,000 guns but was unable to keep up with demand. The success of the firm depended above all on good contacts with the merchants in seaports. They maintained agents and warehouses in London, Liverpool, Bristol and Lancaster. From these warehouses they supplied some of the most prominent and successful English slave traders: Foster Cunliffe, John Tarleton, John/James Parr, Joseph Mannesty (who gave John Newton his first command), Richard Oswald and, not least, Alexander and David Barclay whose banking company – Freame and Barclay – was later to become Barclays Bank.

As the firm developed, it sought out contacts with merchants outside the UK, and maintained an agent in Lisbon. Farmer & Galton found Lisbon a good outlet for their Angola muskets. The firm also had wide contracts with merchants in Nantes, Bordeaux, Rouen, Lille and St Omer. Seeking to diversify its market, the partners also sold muskets to Caribbean planter Assemblies to be used by local militias to put down struggles for freedom by enslaved Africans.

Having amassed a fortune from the 'African trade', the Galton family moved to diversify their business by investing in areas like transport and mining that were to fuel the industrial revolution: Hagley Turnpike Company (Galton Sr), Birmingham Canal Navigation Company (Galton Jr), Warwickshire Canal (Galton Jr), Rose Copper Company (Galton Sr & Jr).

In the 1790s Samuel Galton Jr, a Quaker and member of the Lunar Society, was effectively put on trial by the Society of Friends for "fabricating instruments for the destruction of mankind". Unrepentant, Galton wrote a long epistle that offered the following arguments in his defence:

1. My family have been in the business for 70 years, and I have served the company for 30 years. Why has it taken so long to make this charge?
2. The business was an inheritance that you cannot simply get rid of just like that
3. While doing business, I have fulfilled my duties as a Quaker with the approval of the Society
4. The manufacture of arms does not mean the approbation of 'offensive war'. After all arms can be used legitimately for defensive wars.
5. Don't we all contribute to war by paying taxes to the government to make war?
6. Others are more guilty than I am: "…those who use the produce of the labor of Slaves, as Tobacco, Rum, Sugar, Rice, Indigo, and Cotton, are more intimately, and directly the Promoters of the Slave Trade, than the Vendor of Arms is the Promoter of War;…because the Consumption of these Articles, is the very Ground and Cause of Slavery."

Soon after his suspension from the Society of Friends, Galton moved his remaining gun capital into banking, the Birmingham Bank (later Midland Bank).

Even without the Galton family, Birmingham's 'African trade' continued to flourish, and there was strong local resistance to the abolition of the slave trade. In a House of Commons debate in 1792 it was stated that Birmingham's gun trade depended almost entirely on the African trade in peace time. As late as 1880 some 100,000 to 150,000 flint, bright-barrelled muskets were still being made per annum for the 'African market'.

Below: Gilded statue, by William Bloye, of Boulton, Wattt and Murdoch, Broad Street, Birmingham. Photo: Richard Battye.

JAMES WATT & MATTHEW BOULTON: TOYS AND STEAM ENGINES

In September 2006, Birmingham City Council unveiled the re-gilded statue of Boulton, Watt and Murdoch which had graced the Centenary Square area of the city since 1956. Designed by William Boyce, the statue had been removed for three years to undergo extensive renovation at considerable expense to taxpayers. Today, Matthew Boulton is venerated as a 'father of Birmingham', and preparations are currently in full swing to celebrate the bicentenary of his death in 2009. As members of the Lunar Society, it is Boulton and Watt's contribution to anti-slavery activities that gets highlighted – 'They abhorred slavery' – rather than their contribution to the slave trade and slavery as a result of their business interests. Boulton was a businessman whose wealth derived both from steam engines and 'toys'. Watt, too, came from a Scottish family that had some connection to Glasgow's tobacco trade. Indeed, records show that Watt's father owned a slave and put up some of the money that financed the slave ship, *Perseverance*.

Matthew Boulton started out as a 'toys' manufacturer at Snow Hill. With little room for expansion at the premises that he had inherited from his father, he leased a water-powered rolling mill and house in the village of Handsworth, then located 2 miles from Birmingham, for £1,000 in 1761. At this location he proceeded to build his famous Soho Manufactory in 1762. Here he was joined by a new business partner, John Fothergill.

In the eighteenth century, Birmingham produced a whole range of objects that earned it the soubriquet of

THREE CONTINENTS: ONE HISTORY

> 'I have been considering of the conversation Mr Galton & I had respecting the merits of the Steam Engine as I am going to have some Sugar Works erected in the island in Trinidad. Wish to have your ideas and the opinions of experienc'd people how far it would be practicable to erect them on that plan: the Want of Wind & Water the principle on which they are at present work'd, retards the progress so very much, particularly in crop time, that if an Engine could be invented with a certainty of its answering the purpose, the Rolers so contriv'd that if possible to have a greater effect in the pressing of the Cane than what is at present used….'
>
> Letter from John Dawson to Messrs Watt & Boulton, 9th November 1790.

Soho Manufactory built by Matthew Boulton in 1762. Courtesy of Birmingham Archives & Heritage.

> 'Today I dined with Mr Pennant in Grosvenor Sqr who is a very amiable Man with 10 or 12 thousand £ a year & has the largest estate in Jamaica. There was also Mr Gale & Mr Beeston Long who have two very large sugar plantations there & who wish to see steam answer in lieu of horses.'
>
> Letter from Matthew Boulton London, 17 April 1783.

'the toy-shop of Europe'. Toys then meant something quite different to what we understand today. 200 years ago, 'toys' referred to a very wide variety of small, and often quite fancy, artifacts made in a wide variety of metals: buckles, buttons, corkscrews, seals, snuff boxes, watch chains, sword hilts, and so on.

In Birmingham, the industry was export-oriented. While the main market for toys, particularly the more expensive filigree items was in Europe, Birmingham toys like combs, buckles, and buttons, formed an essential part of the cargoes of slaving ships. In 1759 over 20,000 people were engaged in an industry that produced goods to the value of £600,000 a year, five-sixths of which was exported. As in the case of the gun industry, it is not inconceivable that exports to Europe from companies like Hollier and Tippin might have found their way to Africa aboard French slave ships.

As a representative of the Buckle Makers of Birmingham, Matthew Boulton was already a prominent manufacturer in Birmingham when he joined forces with James Watt to exploit the latter's steam engine invention in 1775. The engine business was organised at the Soho Manufactory, but only a few speclaist parts were manufactured there, the rest being contracted to local founders. With the addition of the new engine foundry, Soho Foundry, in 1795, Boulton felt that he now had the capacity to 'supply the world with engines'.

Through Samuel Galton's prominent links with West Indian planters, Boulton was able to develop a plantation market in steam engines. In 1793 he wrote about a meeting that he had had with three Caribbean planters in London including James Pennant who had amassed a large fortune which he proceeded to invest in North Wales slate quarries. Planters like John Dawson were soon to come calling on Messrs Watt & Boulton. In response, the latter sought to tailor their engine designs to the demands of planters, indicating precisely how enslaved Africans could feed sugar cane into the crusher without risk to the capital invested in either machine or African. Through contacts of the kind described above, the firm Boulton & Watt supplied Caribbean islands with nearly 200 steam engines, designed for sugar mills, between 1778 and 1825.

As the developers of a new technology, Watt & Boulton understood fully well the necessity of providing a one-stop shop of services that would encourage the take up of this expensive new machinery. The firm engaged a number of fitters and engine erectors who could be called upon to erect and maintain the engines. Such was the case of Robert McMurdo who went out to Guyana to erect engines on estates belonging to Thomas Daniel & Son. McMurdo's death while in Guyana led James Watt to express concern that this would put off other fitters and erectors from accepting Caribbean assignments. These foreign contracts were quite lucrative. Kinnear, a fitter and engine erector who worked for the Soho Foundry, went to Demerara for Thomas Daniel & Co. for three years, and earned £200, £250 and £250 respectively plus board, lodging and passage out and back. As part of the contract, he insisted that he would not move beyond four or five miles from the Guyanese coast.

In Britain, refineries were equally quick to adopt the new technology to transform Caribbean muscovado sugar into refined sugar, fit for European consumption.

THE BRASS INDUSTRY

As a city of 'a thousand trades', Birmingham made many other items that entered the African trade. It made the fetters, iron-collars, shackles and padlocks that became standard items of the slave coffle that transported people from the interior of Africa to the coast. On board slaving ships traversing the Middle Passage, Birmingham-made fetters were used to restrain captured Africans to prevent insurrections. On Caribbean plantations, especially in the notorious House of Correction, these objects were transformed into inventive contraptions for crushing resistance amongst the enslaved. A British Anti-Slavery report observed that Birmingham-made collars and shackles were still being exported to Africa in 1840.

The brass trade of Birmingham played a vital role in the life of the city. Perhaps the most significant brass product with which the city became identified was the manilla. Produced by casting, manillas were exported in millions to West Africa where they became a form of money that could be used to exchange for captured Africans.

Above: Model cane crusher designed by Laing & Anderson to enable Boulton & Watt to advertise their steam engine technology to Caribbean planters. Courtesy of Birmingham Archives & Heritage.

'I am sorry to learn the fate of Robert McMurdo, both on his own account, and because it may deter other men from going out to the West Indies, though when the details come to be known it will appear that he has not attended to the advice given him.'

Letter, James Watt Jr to William Creighton, 30 Dec 1815

THREE CONTINENTS: ONE HISTORY

Smaller versions were used ornamentally. Between five and twenty tons of brass wire were exported each year to Ghana and Nigeria in the form of 'guinea rods' of varying thickness. In West Africa they would be used as an exchange medium, or transformed into ornamental bangles or bracelets. Birmingham also exported large quantities of armlet and anklet rings made of brass tubes of varying diameters. To make themselves independent of the brass manufactories from Bristol and Cheadle, Matthew Boulton encouraged the town's brassfounders to build their own smelting and brass houses. With subscriptions of £20,000 the Birmingham Metal Company came into being in 1781, with its headquarters at Brass House 'by ye canal' on Broad Street, which cheapened the transportation of raw materials. The building is now a restaurant.

In sum, Birmingham's connection to the slave trade was a long and important one that contributed to the growth of the town from a population of 25,000 in 1700 to 75,000 at the end of the eighteenth century. Key industries of the city were dependent on the African market.

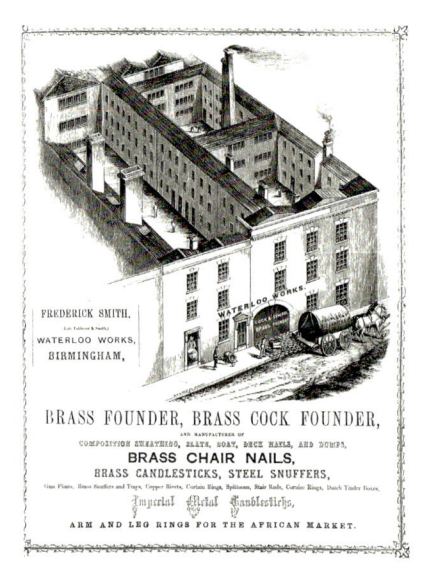

Above: Advertisement, Frederick Smith, brass founder.
Below: Brass House, former headquarters of Birmingham Metal Company.
Right: Adala ankets, Nigeria. These brass anklets were worn by young women who are ready to marry, and also represent wealth. Courtesy Bristol's Museums, Galleries & Archives.

8

West Midlands regiments and the preservation of the Caribbean slave order

Dr Rebecca Condron & Dr Clive Harris

There has never been an empire in history without an accompanying army to defend it. Nowhere was this truer than in the Caribbean where the preservation of the plantation system necessarily required the imposition of a brutal militarised system which had a number of tiers or levels. At the top of this system were the local militia and the British troops. The latter were garrisoned in numerous forts. Over 500 of these forts dot the Caribbean landscape. The fact that forts were generally found on the coast of each island reminds us that British regiments were not there merely to support the local militias in putting down struggles for freedom amongst the enslaved and amongst the Maroon communities that sprung up in many islands. Their fundamental role until the middle of the eighteenth century was to defend/guard the colonial sugar economies of each European country from the predations of rival countries. The Caribbean was a region where a large number of European powers – Britain, Spain, Portugal, Netherlands, France, Denmark-Norway, Sweden, and Latvia – sought to develop their rival colonial empires. The valuable commerce of these colonial empires had to be protected both from slave revolts and from foreign incursions/invasions. Conflict pervaded the region. These conflicts did not simply take place on plantations. Between 1689 and 1815, European countries spent no fewer than 64 years at war.

From the middle of the eighteenth century, maintenance of security on plantations, and by extension domination over and exploitation of Africans, was becoming increasingly problematic because of the changing demography of the islands. As the ratio of enslaved Africans to white owners/masters grew inexorably with the influx of Africans and the growing absenteeism amongst a planter class that retired to England to enjoy its wealth, so too did white fears increase about the danger of rebellions and insurrections among enslaved Africans. Local Assemblies responded by passing legislation designed to increase the number of whites. These were the so-called Deficiency Laws that compelled planters to maintain a permanent ratio of white servants to enslaved Africans under penalty of a fine. By the end of the eighteenth century, maintaining the coercive power and efficiency of the local militia had become extremely difficult without resorting to the admission of groups such as 'coloureds' and free blacks, e.g. Maroons, whose loyalties were always perceived as suspect. The less efficient local militias

Brimstone Hill, St Kitts. A massive fortress built by the British between 1690-1790, using African labour, on 800 foot volcanic plug, to protect island from rival European powers. Photos courtesy of Michael Head.

Right: Kings Head, Bird Street, Lichfield, Staffordshire. Birthplace of 38th Regiment of Foot (South Staffs Regiment). Courtesy of Staffordshire Regiment Museum.

were, the greater was the reliance upon white British troops garrisoned in the islands. (As an aside, one should also acknowledge the significant role of the Royal Navy, given the necessity of moving troops rapidly between islands in the event of a rebellion or foreign attack.)

The attempt by local planters to turn British regiments into a police force was a subject that made the relationship between London and colonial capitals such as Kingston very fraught, particularly when planters remained unwilling to contribute proportionately to the upkeep of troops and to the building and maintenance of garrisons/forts.

THE USE OF BRITISH REGIMENTS

British regiments themselves were an important feat of social engineering. Not only did they constitute the space for forging a sense of Britishness from the different social strata and disparate nationalities that constituted the United Kingdom after the Act of Union of 1707, but these social strata and nationalities were brought into a web of power whose single aim was to bend the will of the African to that of the European. Colour was the social glue that allowed social divisions to be transcended. The outcome was the production of a Britannia that sought to rule the waves while insisting that it could never be subordinated to the status of slave that it imposed on others. In effect Britannia became a white ship kept afloat by the sinews of black bodies.

The key regiments from the Birmingham hinterland that allowed Britannia to rule the waves in the Caribbean were the following:

- 36th Regiment of Foot or the 1st Herefordshire Regiment
- 53rd Regiment of Foot or the Shropshire Regiment
- 64th Regiment of Foot or the North Staffordshire Regiment
- 38th Regiment of Foot or the South Staffordshire Regiment
- 6th Regiment of Foot or 1st Warwickshire Regiment
- 29th Regiment of Foot or 1st Worcestershire Regiment

Our interest is in the last four which recruited in Birmingham and the areas immediately adjacent after county designations were introduced in 1782 to increase local affiliation, and thereby expand recruitment.

Formed as Sir Walter Vane's Regiment of Foot, the 6th Foot recruited so successfully in the county in which Birmingham was located (Warwickshire) in 1778, that it was called 'The Warwickshire'. Birmingham supplied the largest proportion of the men, and raised £2,000 by public subscription for regimental equipment (*Showell's Dictionary of Birmingham*). As early as 1778, three companies of the 6th Foot were stationed at Warwick, four at Birmingham, two at Stratford and three at Coventry, making it truly a Midlands outfit. Marching Orders logged by the War Office show a regular presence by the 6th in the town of Birmingham. Also located nearby was the 1st Volunteer Battalion of the South Staffordshire. They had their headquarters in the Handsworth area of Birmingham, which was then not part of the city but a parish in the County of Staffordshire.

During the eighteenth century, formal army recruitment centres did not exist and general conscription did not take place in Britain until the Great War. Instead, mobile recruiting parties, consisting of a Sergeant and a Drummer Boy, were set up in towns and villages, usually in inns and taverns, where strong ale and wholesome food were offered to the many impoverished and/or unemployed. In this way, some local men were attracted into the army by the lure of food and money. Others were plied with alcohol and tricked into making an enlistment pledge. Sometimes a 'King's Shilling' was placed in the bottom of an ale tankard. Once the unsuspecting drinker had the shilling in his mouth, he was considered enlisted, having accepted the payment. In these diverse ways, Colonel Lillingston's 38th Regiment of Foot (later known as the South Staffordshire Regiment) came into existence at the Kings Head in Bird Street, Lichfield, on 25th March 1705. It is possible too that, in a time of national shortages of recruits, more sinister methods of recruitment such as kidnapping or crimping (the army equivalent of press-ganging) would have been utilised.

The 38th Regiment of Foot has one of the longest highest histories of British regimental service in the Caribbean. In 1707, it left for Antigua which was to become its headquarters for the next 57 years. Forgotten, ill-equipped and half-starved, the regiment guarded the Leeward Islands, fighting the French, warding off pirates and assisting local island militias in putting down rebellions by enslaved Africans. In 1739, on the outbreak of war with Spain, a detachment was sent to attack the Spanish territory of Venezuela. Similar wars with France led to detachments being sent to Guadeloupe (1759) and Martinique (1762). Before the Haitian Revolutionary period, the 6th Regiment of Foot or 1st Warwickshire Regiment had early tours of duty in the Caribbean that took it to Jamaica (1703 and 1742), St Kitts (1742), and St Vincent (1772-76) where it was used to subdue the native Kalinago people and facilitate British take over of the island. The 29th Regiment of Foot or 1st Worcestershire Regiment had only one period of active service in the Caribbean (Jamaica, 1740-41) before the Haitian Revolutionary period. The Worcestershire, South Staffordshire and 1st Warwickshire regiments were to play a critical role in the Caribbean during the French Revolutionary Wars of the 1790s.

> 'We have the pleasure to inform the public that the scheme set on foot by Lord Warwick and afterwards approved by the King and Ministry for raising troops in the present emergency, meets with the entire approbation of the principal inhabitants of Coventry, Warwick and Birmingham; and that a great number of the nobility, gentry, clergy and inhabitants of the county at large have signified their readiness to support a measure which tends so much to the good of the public…. and His Majesty has given orders that the Officers etc, shall march into Warwickshire, as soon as the subscriptions are opened, for the raising of the recruits. When the corps is complete, it will for ever bear the distinguished title of THE WARWICKSHIRE REGIMENT'.
>
> **Coventry Mercury, 2nd February 1778.**

> 'French émigrés are flocking to (British Islands) from Martinique and Guadeloupe, where, they apprehend, the same Game will be played as has been at San Domingo. I am particularly cautious in admitting any Negroes from the above islands, to prevent if possible, inculcating the principles and doctrines among our slaves, which they have so fatally imbibed in their own islands, and have given directions for many who have been already admitted with their masters, to be sent back'.
>
> Governor William Woodley, St Christopher, December 1792.

CAMPAIGNS OF THE HAITIAN REVOLUTIONARY PERIOD (1791-1804)

The role that the British forces played in the Caribbean during the (Saint Domingue) Haitian Revolutionary period is varied. The coincidence with the French Revolutionary Wars meant that the troops sometimes adopted an offensive position in an attempt to take French islands or bases that were strategically important both to France and to Britain. They also undertook interventionist roles in an attempt to put down or prevent rebellions by enslaved Africans or Maroons.

The arrival of refugees fleeing the Haitian revolution soon made Jamaican planters extremely anxious that events happening in the nearby French territory could spill over into other parts of the Caribbean. Refugees brought with them lurid tales of destruction of property and uprisings amongst the enslaved Africans and 'mulattos' (mixed population). For many white Haitian planters, salvation lay in asking Britain to intervene and take over the island. The increasing radicalisation of the French Revolution – the beheading of the King and the declaration of a republic proclaiming the rights and liberties of 'men' – had an impact not only in Birmingham but also in the French territories of the Caribbean. Britain dithered in trying to decide how best to cordon off the dangerous ideas of 'liberty, equality and fraternity'. Eventually it decided to step in by using the capitulation agreement signed by exiled Haitian planters purporting to represent the island. Under this agreement, sovereignty of St Domingue was temporarily surrendered to the British pending the restoration of the French monarchy. The local Commander in Chief, Governor Williamson of Jamaica, was authorised in 1793 to send an expeditionary force of 700 from Jamaica to Haiti. This arrived on the 19th September 1793. The diminution of the Jamaican garrison was vociferously opposed by white Jamaican planters who argued that it left the island unprotected. Anticipating the British invasion, the French Republican Commissioner in Haiti, Leger-Felicité Sonthonax, pre-emptively proclaimed slave emancipation in the territory in August 1793 in order to make Haiti impossible to take over. With this proclamation, the basis was laid for a realignment of forces to confront an external enemy committed to the restoration of the status quo ante, i.e. slavery. Flushed from victories in central Haiti, Toussaint soon deserted the Spanish army, which had come across the border with a promise of freedom after the conclusion of hostilities, to realign himself with the French. He turned on the Spanish and drove them from the island in 1795.

British forces had some initial successes as Royalist forces came over to their side. However, others from whom the British sought support stood aside in the absence of any specific mention of equal rights and privileges in the capitulation agreement. Recognising that only black troops had the capacity to engage in the kind of guerrilla warfare that prevailed in Haiti, Williamson sought to raise two legions of black/'mulatto' troops but was hamstrung by the fact that he was forbidden by London to grant a similar promise of freedom – at the end of service – as the French had done with their emancipation proclamation. The inability to promise freedom even at the end of service created an ideological divide which placed Britain on the side of preserving slavery, and led to the melting away of black and 'mulatto' support. On the strength of promised reinforcements from the United Kingdom, Williamson raided the Jamaican garrison and took a further 500 soldiers to compensate for the level

64th, SECOND STAFFORDSHIRE REGIMENT, 1802.
(FOREIGN SERVICE DRESS, WEST INDIES.)

Officer and men of the 64th Regiment of Foot (Second Staffs Regiment) in foreign service dress, West Indies, 1802. Courtesy of Staffordshire Regiment Museum.

of mortality already being encountered (leaving behind only 1500 troops to defend Jamaica).

The arrival in the Caribbean of the Grey-Jervis Expeditionary Force in January 1794 did not offer an immediate relief. Arriving as it did eight weeks later than planned, this meant that most of the fighting would take place not in the optimum fighting season (November – March) but in what was called the 'sickly season', that period between May and October when heavy rains fall, the heat intensifies and when non-immune troops were exposed to the dangers of contracting sub-tropical diseases such as yellow fever. The Expedition was composed of some 7,000 British troops plus 800 enslaved black rangers. The 64th (North Staffs), 29th (Worcestershire), and 6th (1st Warwicks) were part of this campaign. General Sir Charles Grey (later Earl Grey)'s plan was to go south with the

Officer and Sargeant, Dalzells (later 38th Regiment), West Indies, 1742. Courtesy of Staffordshire Regiment Museum.

trade winds to Barbados to replenish supplies, then sweep north to cut off French economic and military strength at its knees by taking the French Antilles, starting with Martinique – where the important French naval base of Port Royal was located – go back to pick up the less important island of St Lucia. He would then go north to Guadeloupe, and then westwards towards Haiti.

In March 1794, the 6th Foot (Warwickshire) and the 64th Foot (Staffordshire) were among the regiments that landed on the strategically important island of Martinique. Not only would its capture destroy the morale of the French troops, and boost that of the British, but it would mean that French supplies would find it harder to get through to other colonies. Deprived of a naval base, it would be difficult for France to sustain a naval presence 5,000 miles from Europe let alone send reinforcements to defend its territories.

Success in Martinique, however, raised a thorny issue that was to bedevil the campaign, namely, how to distribute the prize money that, according to British law, officers were able to claim as their own. Prize-money was important to those who led the troops; the promise of a plentiful 'bounty' was one of the tools that had been used by the British government to entice newly appointed Officers to begin recruitment drives in towns such as Birmingham. Prize-money entitled the Expedition to all arms, ammunition and ships captured from the enemy and also to the property of the conquered islands. A Staffordshire recruit, George Wilkes Unett, who saw extended service in the West Indies with the Royal Artillery during the late eighteenth and early nineteenth centuries wrote to his brother, John Wilkes Unett, a founder member of the Birmingham Law Society and a property developer in Smethwick, in May, 1809, about the large rewards he anticipated to get from the capture of the Les Isles Saintes: "We brought away all the brass guns, powder, flour, which with the 74 gunship, will make altogether about £80,00 to be divided amongst us."

It is thought that some officers of higher ranks used this prize-money to purchase property in the Caribbean and become slave owners themselves. Major George Lucas, for example, of the 38th Regiment, who died in 1747, became a wealthy land owner and slaver with property in the West Indies and southern USA. The ruthlessness and greed displayed by the commanders of the expedition, Grey and Jervis, in claiming the booty as prize-money, created a furore in London that damaged their personal reputations and that of the

British forces in the West Indies.

Despite the greed, the operation in Martinique was a military success, after a five-week struggle for Fort Bourbon, in which the 6th Foot played a role (both the 64th and 6th Regiments were awarded battle honours for their role in Martinique). The joint land and sea operation finally forced the French General Rochambeau to surrender in the face of depleted arms, food and water and with a numerically weak and demoralized army. A detachment of the 64th (North Staffs) was left behind as a garrison. In the campaign, the British army had lost 92 men in five weeks of battle, while 228 were wounded and three missing. The largest loss of life, however, was to come not from fighting but from disease.

As the Expedition sailed towards St Lucia, the naval commander, Jervis, was already speaking alarmingly about the severe losses of men from 'fever and fluxes' (i.e. dysentery). The Expedition arrived in St Lucia on April 1st 1794. The island fell in five days, without adding to the loss of British life. A detachment of the 6th (Warwicks) was left behind for garrison duty before the Expedition headed north to take Guadeloupe, capturing Les Isles Saintes on the way. Guadeloupe was swiftly captured in a campaign that resulted in the loss of 15 men (and two missing). Both the 6th and 64th Foot sent two companies to Guadeloupe from among their ranks but the majority were garrisoned on St Lucia and Martinique, respectively.

Between March and October, 1794, the 6th Regiment's monthly returns, held in the War Office records in the National Archives, show that each month between 81 and 119 men were out of action due to sickness, some still in quarters but the majority severe enough to be admitted to hospital, while the report for June shows that, in just one month, 40 of its number had died. The 64th Foot fared worse: Before any swords had even been drawn, 348 men were already sick, leaving seven dead and just 212 present and fit for duty, while the returns for July 1794 show 84 dead and for September, 72.

Despite the successes of the Windward-Leeward campaign, the Grey-Jervis Expedition found itself so considerably depleted by death, illness or garrison duties that it was not in a position to mount a significant attack on the prize of the French Caribbean, Saint Domingue (Haiti). Nevertheless, recognising the need to assist the Haitian invasion campaign, a detachment of 1700 men was sent to Haiti under General Whyte in May 1794 in anticipation that back-up would soon arrive from other European theatres of war. This backup did not materialise. The British Haitian commander, General Williamson, used the detachments to take the capital, Port-au-Prince, but without further reinforcements, the invasion force could not push on.

The conundrum for the Expedition was quite simple: how to take islands and retain them given the levels of mortality experienced. The conundrum had to be addressed immediately when, the rest of the fleet having trundled north to St Kitts, it was learned in June 1794 that French troops under the command of Victor Hugues (a Commissioner of the Republican Convention) have arrived in the Caribbean with a proclamation abolishing slavery in all French territories (i.e. as opposed to the partial proclamation already issued in Haiti by Sonthanax) that admitted Africans to full privileges. With the support of local people, Hugues proceeded to rout the British garrison left behind in the capital of southern Guadeloupe. Grey rushed back to Guadeloupe but to no avail.

> 'There is a sad ugly fever here – the artillery are healthy, but the 2nd battalion 68th Regiment that disembarked two days ago are very sickly. I cannot tell you how many are dead within these 48 hours. When they came on shore one died in the boat and three were left on the wharf in the last agonies – our Garrison is now above 2000 men – so many coming at once, has put us into dreadful confusion – my heart aches for what I see going on. I never was cut out for a soldier, and I wish to God I had done with it'
>
> **Richard Wilkes Unett (Barbados) to John Unett (Birmingham), 25th Sept 1802.**

> 'A man deserves everything he can get in this diabolical country – mine is literally got the sweat of my brows for at this moment the perspiration is running down me in torrents in every direction. The weather has been and still is excessively hot – I have heard some of the natives say, lately, that they never felt the weather so warm – I declare in riding out in the middle of the day, which I am often obliged to do, the Sun almost melts one alive. When I came out to this country, it was understood that there would be a general relief of the Companies in the West Indies this Xmas – This plan is now dropped there being not artillery sufficient in England to furnish the relief this year…
> We have had a terrible Fever here, which carried off eight or ten soldiers in a day – sometimes only after one day's illness. Poor Lt Stanwix of the Arty who came out with me, caught the fever on his passage from Mart/que – was landed here one day – the next we buried him, after three days' sickness. Thank ~God it has now subsided in this island, tho at Dominique, Martinique, Trinidad & Guadeloupe the mortality is dreadful – The French have lost at the latter island in three months, out of 3500 men – 3300 men!!! Only about 200 men alive about a month ago – in all probability those are dead by this time…. They have buried by the last accounts in this oountry forty three Generals & Field Officers out of seventy!!!'
>
> **Richard Wilkes Unett to John Unett,
> 21st Oct 1802.**

Instead, he was forced to relinquish both Grande Terre and Basse Terre. The repulse of the British in Guadeloupe was to send a very clear signal to opposition forces in other islands that British occupation could be challenged. Without reinforcements from the United Kingdom, the Grey-Jervis Expedition had effectively run into the sand. Of the original 7,000 men only 2,000 were fit for service; 1,200 were sick; the rest dead. Adding to this naval and transport losses, and the losses from existing garrisons, it is estimated that 12,000 British men lost their lives in the Caribbean in 1794 alone.

The situation began to get even more precipitous when Jervis was informed about the reversals that had taken place in the islands that the Expedition had recently conquered. St Lucia, with a sizeable French community, was in open revolt and British forces had retreated to the capital, Castries. Grenada too has gone the same way, with troops withdrawn to a small cordon around the capital, St Georges. Under the leadership of a mulatto planter, Fédon, enslaved Africans and radical French – supplied with arms and stores by Victor Hugues in Guadeloupe – had taken over the rest of the island. The Expeditionary Commander, Jervis, also learned that the Black Caribs in St Vincent whose lands had been stolen in the British campaign of 1772-3 had seized the opportunity to take back the island from white planters. British forces were penned in in Fort Charlotte and the capital, Kingstown.

Recognising the limitations of the rag-tag reinforcements composed of foreign (German, Dutch) mercenaries, deserters, criminals and young boys sent out from the United Kingdom in March 1795, Commander Jervis set about raising a black regiment without waiting for approval from London. He returned to St Lucia in April 1795. The campaign to retake the island failed and high mortality from yellow fever and the guerrilla campaign of what was derisively called the 'brigands' forced Grey to evacuate the island on 18th June 1795. It is at this stage that Jamaica entered the fray with the outbreak of the Maroon War in July 1795. Troops that were destined for Haiti now had to stay in Jamaica to fight the Maroons. It took five months to subdue the Maroons. In December 1795, the main (Trelawny) Maroon group was defeated and transported to Nova Scotia and thence to Sierra Leone.

In 1796 relief finally came in the shape of the Abercrombie expedition, 20,000 troops sent from Europe. Again, instead of being able to take Haiti, they were forced into defensive operations. St Lucia was recovered in May 1796 and made secure by leaving behind a large force of 4,000. A month later in Grenada, where another Haiti seemed imminent, the rebellion was put down though Fedon was never captured. British troops were successful too in St Vincent, particularly with the willingness of planters to do the unthinkable and raise a corps of black rangers (later to become the 1st West India Regiment). The insurrection was decisively broken in November 1796 and 5,000 'Black Caribs' were deported to Central America four months later.

Despite its successes, the new Abercrombie Expedition had lost half of its forces by the start of 1797. According to Fortescue, between 1794 and 1796 over 40,000 troops had died, and a similar number had been discharged from the service from wounds and other infirmities. They died from the fighting; they died of typhoid contracted during the passage across the Atlantic; they died of malaria and yellow fever, contracted in the

Caribbean; and they died from the 'new' rum – contaminated with poisonous lead and fusel oil by the distilling process – that they drank in the belief that it would prevent them from contracting yellow fever. It was a massive squandering of life. The 6th Foot, the 64th and the 29th Foot returned to England mere skeletons of the regiments that had left British shores less than two years earlier. The heavy losses suffered ensured that, although they would continue to be the Warwickshire, Staffordshire and Worcestershire Regiments in name, they would never again recruit heavily in the West Midlands in the future.

Declaration of war by Spain in 1796 suddenly opened out new theatres of war in the Caribbean, e.g. Trinidad, for the Abercrombie Expedition to deal with. With the cost of the Haitian campaign spiralling out of control, and Toussaint now firmly ensconced as Commander-in-Chief of French Forces in Saint Domingue, the British government came to the view that the island could not be taken. The irresistible campaign launched by the forces commanded by Toussaint L'Ouverture to drive British forces from the island in early 1798, forced General Maitland to sue for peace with Toussaint to secure the unmolested evacuation of the remnants of British forces from the island. By the beginning of October 1798 all British forces had withdrawn from the island.

BLACK TROOPS: A DANGEROUS SOLUTION?

With the dream of maritime domination shattered, and with the British army strung out in defensive garrisons across the Caribbean islands, and a British public war-weary and highly critical of the high mortality amongst troops (51 percent!), a new warfare strategy had to be developed for the Caribbean region. The germ of the strategy had already been apparent in the low mortality amongst African troops used throughout the campaigns of the Haitian revolutionary period, in their greater adaptability to the kind of warfare that prevailed in the region, and in the willingness of other European nations to make use of them. This strategy centred on commissioning twelve black West India regiments between 1794 and 1802 – almost half the British Caribbean garrison. Recruitment was however a major problem. With the immediate crisis over, planters refused to supply enslaved Africans for military service, fearing that this would destroy the fundamental distinction between black and white that it was essential to maintain. Perforce, the Army had to become the biggest purchaser of Africans in the final years of British Slave Trade. Indeed, it is significant that abolitionists such as Pitt went very quiet on the need to abolish the slave trade faced with the army's demand for enslaved Africans. When war resumed in 1803, after the temporary truce of the Treaty of Amiens, black troops were to play an increasingly important role in the (re)conquest of the Dutch, Spanish, Danish and French territories in 1803-5, 1807-10 and in 1815.

When the 1807 Slave Trade Abolition Act was passed, the Army continued to acquire Africans 'liberated' from slaving ships of other countries. The increasing recognition that the putting down of rebellions by Africans who were themselves not free represented a fundamental contradiction led to the passing of 1807 Mutiny Act which offered 10,000 African recruits their freedom on the condition they could never be discharged into civil society. In addition, careful attention was paid to always maintaining a white officer corps, emphasising the superiority of army life over life on the plantation, and keeping an eye on where Africans were recruited.

REGIMENTS BY LOCATION & YEAR

REGIMENT	ISLAND	YEAR
Warwicks	Jamaica	1703
Warwicks	Jamaica	1742
Warwicks	St Kitts	1742
Warwicks	St Vincent	1772-76
Warwicks	St Vincent	1793
Warwicks	Barbados	1793-94
Warwicks	Guadeloupe	1794
Warwicks	Martinique	1794
Warwicks	St Lucia	1794
Warwicks	Trinidad	1864
Warwicks	Jamaica	1864-65
Herefords	Jamaica	1741-43
Herefords	Jamaica	1764-73
Herefords	Barbados	1830
Herefords	Antigua	1833
Herefords	St Lucia	1834
Herefords	Barbados	1837
Herefords	Barbados	1851
Herefords	Trinidad	1852
Herefords	Tobago	1852
Herefords	Barbados	1853
Herefords	St Vincent	1853
Herefords	Grenada	1853
Herefords	Jamaica	1854
Staffs	Antigua	1707-64
Staffs	Guadeloupe	1759
Staffs	Martinique	1762
Staffs	Guadeloupe	1794
Staffs	Martinique	1794
Staffs	Barbados	1796-97
Staffs	Surinam	1804-13
Staffs	St Lucia	1803
Staffs	Virgin Islands	1801
Worcesters	Jamaica	1740-1
Worcesters	Grenada	1795-96
Worcesters	St Lucia	1831-38
Worcesters	Antigua	1831-38
Worcesters	Barbados	1831-38
Worcesters	Jamaica	1851-56
Worcesters	Trinidad	1851-56
Worcesters	Barbados	1870-72
Shropshires	St Lucia	1796
Shropshires	St Vincent	1797-97
Shropshires	Trinidad	1797
Shropshires	St Vincent	1799
Shropshires	Martinique	1801

9

The Lunar Society in Birmingham and its role in the Abolition of the Slave Trade

Dr Rebecca Condron

This book goes some way to establishing that the struggle to end the slave trade and slavery in no way sprouted from a few privileged men in parliament, as the 2007 commemorations may have led many of us to believe. On the contrary, the continuous battle by enslaved Africans to liberate themselves, through resistance, revolution and rebellion, was paramount in bringing about the need for an end to the system. This point has been discussed extensively in Chapter five.

In eighteenth century Britain, there was a different kind of effort taking place, an effort to educate others in the realities of the horrors of slavery and one which ultimately aimed to force the government to push forward a parliamentary bill to abolish the slave trade. We have heard of the abolitionists and we may even be able to name a handful of them, such as Thomas Clarkson or Granville Sharpe and recently we have become more familiar with the contribution of the African abolitionist, Olaudah Equiano. We may also be aware of the sort of tactics the abolitionists used in order to publicize the movement: pamphlets and talks; research; boycotts; court hearings and petitions. If we do, much of this information probably relates to what was happening in other parts of the country, and particularly in London, but very rarely do we discover how Birmingham contributed to the abolition movement.

In Chapter ten I discuss how women in Birmingham attempted to help put an end to slavery in the 1820s and 1830s, at a time when the trade had been outlawed but the practice was still very much in force. However, the subject of the trade in human beings on such a massive scale was being discussed in the town of Birmingham, and surrounding areas, decades before the foundation of the Birmingham Ladies' Society for the Relief of British Negro Slaves. In this chapter, it is on a handful of men who belonged to a group known as the Lunar Society that we focus.

Matthew Boulton, industrialist. Courtesy of Birmingham Archives & Heritage.

THE LUNAR SOCIETY

And better in th'untimely grave to rot,
The world and its all its cruelties forgot,
Than, dragg'd once more beyond the Western main,
To groan beneath some dastard planter's chain,
Where my poor countrymen in bondage wait
The slow enfranchisement of ling'ring fate.
Oh! my heart sinks, my dying eyes o'erflow,
When mem'ry paints the picture of their woe!
For I have seen them, ere the dawn of day,
Rouz'd by the lash, begin their chearless way;
Greeting with groans unwelcome morn's return,
While rage and shame their gloomy bosoms burn;

Thomas Day, The Dying Negro, 1773

Above: James Watt, industrialist. Courtesy of Birmingham Archives & Heritage.
Below: Soho House, Hansworth, residence of Matthew Boulton and home of the Lunar Society.

Formed in 1775, the Lunar Society was made up of a group of wealthy, educated men who met in Birmingham, at around the end of the eighteenth century, to discuss scientific, cultural and technical matters. They were innovative men with different skills and backgrounds who made headway with new inventions and (not always accepted) ways of thinking. Among its prominent members were the physicist, Joseph Priestley; the philanthropist and Writer, Thomas Day; The Potter, Josiah Wedgewood; the botanist, Erasmus Darwin; the gun manufacturer, Samuel Galton Jnr.; and the businessmen and engineers, Matthew Boulton and James Watt. Some of these are names which we can still find on Birmingham's streets, buildings and structures – Galton Bridge or Matthew Boulton College, for example.

The Lunar Society, so-called because it met on the full-moon (lighting was scarce then and the moon lit the way to make the journey easier), often gathered at Soho House in Handsworth, the home of Matthew Boulton, owner of the impressive metal works, Soho Foundry. The men discussed many contemporary issues including the slave trade and slavery. The slave trade was still an extremely profitable business in Great Britain and, as we shall see, although the Lunar men voiced opposition to it, some played a very ambiguous role in the whole affair, making huge sums of money through the trade in enslaved Africans, not as slavers but as businessmen.

Like their contemporaries, such as those who had formed the Society for the Abolition of the Slave Trade in London, the Lunar men did not call for the abolition of slavery but only of the trade. The logic was that if the supply of African men, women and children to the Caribbean were cut off, then slavery would have to come to a natural end (it was an erroneous supposition!). Perhaps as importantly, the abolitionists believed that a bill to

> 'Some Europeans, finding Negro slaves in this wretched degraded condition, to which they themselves have reduced them, have had the assurance, and the folly, to pronounce them to be a species of men greatly inferior to themselves. But were the Europeans treated in the same manner a sufficient length of time, it is demonstrable that the most intelligent of them would be no better. Those who see Negroes in their native country, or in circumstances of better treatment among ourselves, are satisfied that they are by no means inferior to Europeans in point of understanding. According to the observations of a late ingenious traveller, the ancient Egyptians so famed for their wisdom, were the very same people with the present Negroes'.
>
> **Joseph Priestley,**
> **Sermon against the Slave Trade, 1788.**

Above: Joseph Priestly, physicist. Courtesy of Birmingham Archives & Heritage.

end to the trade would be more likely to make it through parliament where, after all, sat so many planters, merchants and company directors who needed slavery for their own financial well being. This wealth was not only of the utmost importance to planters and the like, but it was also vital to the coffers of the British Government!

That the members of the Lunar Society had different ideas about the slave trade is evident from analysing a few of the individuals belonging to it. It should be remembered that this was not an anti-slavery society but a type of debating club that merely discussed the trade as one of many issues affecting society at that time. And so, while some worked hard to educate and to propagandise, others felt that they had far too much to loose by fully supporting abolition.

THE LUNAR ABOLITIONISTS

Those Lunar men whose actions demonstrated their commitment to working towards the abolition of the slave trade included Josiah Wedgewood, Thomas Day, Erasmus Darwin and Joseph Priestley. Day's poem, 'The Dying Negro' (previous page), was a very early example of literature being used to break the silence about slavery. Based on a true account of the frustrated love affair between an enslaved African man and a white female servant, and the man's resulting suicide, it was Day's first of many literary assaults on slavery. Likewise, his friend and fellow poet (and much more besides), Darwin, went on to slam the trade in human beings, most notably in his lengthy The Botanic Garden, written between 1789 and 1791. His home in Lichfield was one of the more frequent meeting places of the Society.

The Staffordshire potter Josiah Wedgewood also used his creativity in his support of the abolition movement. In designing a cameo that is still recognisable today, Wedgewood brought the 'slavery discussion' into many homes and meeting places across Britain. Originally commissioned by the Society for the Suppression of the Slave Trade, Wedgewood's work became a symbol of the abolition movement and could be found on many fashion items, including brooches and cuff links. The image is of an enslaved African kneeling as if begging for mercy: the shackled man asks 'Am I Not a Man and a Brother?' Even though the image intended to, and succeeded in, awakening people to the horrors of the slave trade, it does seem to portray the African as a victim rather than as a player in his own anti-slavery struggle (and makes no mention of the millions of enslaved women and children!). Nonetheless, Wedgewood's work was an accessory that became synonymous with the abolition movement in Britain and beyond, working in rather the same way that Oxfam's Make Poverty History bracelets do in the twenty first century. It is of note that, a friend of Thomas Clarkson, Wedgewood was also a shareholder in the Sierra Leone Company which attempted to create a colony for free slaves on the West African coast.

Fellow Lunar man Joseph Priestley also took a prominent role in the abolition movement and, in Birmingham, in 1788, he gave a sermon that was then published as a Sermon against the Slave Trade. In it, he spoke out against the mental and physical suffering of enslaved Africans and he stressed the slavers' role in the degradation of women and the separation of families. Even more unusually he promoted racial equality, a subject rarely touched upon in the 1700s. Such outspoken and controversial opinions made Priestley very unpopular with the powers-that-be and his radical viewpoints won him the reputation as a dangerous dissenter and revolutionary. His home and laboratory at Fair Hill were destroyed by the mob in Birmingham's 1791 riots (sometimes referred to as the 'Priestly Riots'). As a result, he fled to the USA to live out his final years.

It is evident that some prominent and powerful men living in Birmingham and Staffordshire, such as Priestley, Wedgewood and Darwin, did use their particular skills and influence when trying to enlighten others about the slave trade, slavery and the abolition movement. It was not true of all members of the Lunar Society, however, and three, in particular, stand out as men whose personal, that is financial, interests could not be reconciled with their conscience.

THE LUNAR WOULD-BE ABOLITIONISTS

In 1789, Olaudah Equiano had published his *Interesting Narrative*, which told of his experiences as a man captured in Africa, enslaved in the Caribbean and living as a free man in England. The promotion of his *Narrative* led him to Birmingham, where many notable persons had already subscribed to his work, including the Lloyd banking family and The Lunar Society member Joseph Priestley. Two other Lunar men could be found on his list of subscribers – Matthew Boulton and Samuel Galton Jnr., both of whom welcomed Equiano to Birmingham.

The gun manufacturing business of the Galton family is discussed in Chapter seven. The head of the company at this time was Lunar man, Samuel Galton Jnr., a subscriber to Equiano's *Narrative* and furthermore a Quaker, that religious group that had long been opposed to slavery (in fact the Quakers presented the first abolition petitions to the British Parliament in 1783). Galton was not alone in confusing morality and business. One of the men there to welcome Equiano on his brief sojourn to Birmingham was Matthew Boulton, the locally-based businessman and engineer who, alongside his Scottish partner, the engineer James Watt, had designed and patented the steam engine, a machine that could prove invaluable on the sugar plantations in the Caribbean. Boulton's Birmingham Mint also produced the currency to be used in Sierra Leone, where Africans from the Americas were resettled.

That Watt was outspoken against the slave trade is evident from his letter to Messrs Beguye & Co., written less than three months after the start of the uprising in Haiti (Saint Domingue). In this correspondence, Watt damned slavery as "so disgraceful to humanity" and he yearned for its abolition. The duplicity of their thoughts and actions is plain. Sometimes, it seems, 'the right thing to do' had no role in money-making. Galton, Boulton and Watt are clear examples of eighteenth century men who let their love of business outweigh their love for their fellow man.

Be they philanthropists, creative men or businessmen, members of The Lunar Society had something to say about the slave trade and some even had a role in it. While some fought for the good of mankind, others fought for the good of themselves. It is surely a picture that was replicated the island over. There were men and women in Britain who wanted to play some part in halting the injustices of the slave trade, and ultimately slavery, be it through raising money or awareness for the cause. There were also those who, even if they had some moral grievance about the plight of millions of Africans, would not let that get in the way of a personal financial gain. Birmingham had its very own heroes and anti-heroes in the form of The Lunar Society.

Medallion by Josiah Wedgewood.

Gentlemen
    The late unpropitious news from St. Domingo has made us suspend the prosecution of the order for your Engine until we hear from you. We have written to the foundry for that purpose & expect that no material expense has yet been incurred.
    We thought it our duty to give you this information, to relieve part of your anxiety in case any fatal accident should have befallen your friend Mr. Bertrand.
    We sincerely condole with the unhappy sufferers, though we heartily pray that the system of slavery so disgraceful to humanity were abolished by prudent though progressive measures.

We remain etc.
Boulton & Watt.

Letter to the Nantes-based company Messrs Beguye & Co., 31 October 1791.

10

Woman to Woman: The Birmingham Female Society for the Relief of British Negro Slaves

Dr Rebecca Condron

Title page from The First Report of The Female Society... 1826. Courtesy of Birmingham Archives & Heritage.

Throughout 2007, the British public has borne witness to myriad events to commemorate the bi-centenary of the 1807 parliamentary act to abolish the British slave trade. The Royal Mint launched a commemorative £2 coin dedicated to the Act and the Royal Mail devoted a stamp to its 200th anniversary. The film, *Amazing Grace*, charted the life of William Wilberforce MP and his role in the abolition movement, while numerous terrestrial and digital radio and TV stations have aired countless programmes available for general consumption. Exhibitions have taken place in those cities, such as Liverpool, Bristol, London and Hull, which have had historically well-known business, abolitionist or parliamentary links to the Slave Trade; Liverpool hosts the International Slavery Museum. Other cities, not usually associated with the trade (or slavery itself), have staged events that deal with plight of enslaved Africans – Edinburgh, Leeds, Newcastle, Nottingham, Leicester and Glasgow to name but a few. Birmingham itself has hosted such ambitious projects as 'Unshackled', 'The Equiano Project', 'Interwoven Freedom', 'Three Continents, One History', 'Routes to Freedom' and 'Connecting Histories'.

While many of these localised commemorative acts have realised the role played by enslaved Africans in their own freedom, through resistance, rebellion and revolution or by 'Joe Public' in the domestic abolition movement, many national projects have simply opted to evidence the importance of a few 'key' figures, such as Wilberforce and William Pitt PM, in the struggle. Some of these have even taken a celebratory tone, omitting the fact that, although the slave trade was abolished in 1807, slavery itself continued to benefit Britain for at least another 30 years, while the practice was still alive in some countries well into the 1880s (Cuba and Brazil for example).

This chapter, drawing on both original research undertaken as part of the 'Three Continents, One History' project and a study of secondary sources, pieces together the role that the women of Birmingham played in the abolition movement after 1807. Examining the life and work of Mary Prince, it questions how well local women actually understood, and how they related to, enslaved African women, in particular. After all, what could these privileged, mostly wealthy women living in England really know about the lives of so many unheard voices and so many unseen faces thousands of miles away in the Caribbean?

THE FOUNDATION OF THE FEMALE SOCIETY FOR THE RELIEF OF BRITISH NEGRO SLAVES IN BIRMINGHAM

The Female Society for the Relief of British Negro Slaves, which here is abbreviated to BFS (Birmingham Female Society), was founded in Birmingham in 1825. A middle-class female response to the exclusion of women in the British political process, the BFS was not only the first such society to be set up and run by women in Britain, leading the way for so many more similar societies, but it also became the largest. Between its foundation and the act to abolish slavery in 1834, the BFS was the prototype for 73 such associations that aimed to educate others in their campaign for abolition. In its own words of its First Report in 1826, it was the vehicle of:

> A few individuals… who particularly felt for the degraded condition of their own sex … determined to endeavour to awaken (at least in the bosom of English women) a deep and lasting compassion, not only for the bodily sufferings of female slaves but for their moral degradation

And it resolved:

> That we form ourselves into a Society for the melioration of the condition of the unhappy children of Africa, and especially of Female Negro Slaves, who, living under the British dominion, receive from British hands their lot of bitterness

Initially, the Society aimed to alert women in England to the realities of slavery and to illustrate the horrors that enslaved African women, in particular, were being subjected to by their English (and so, Christian) 'masters' and 'owners'. It hoped that by promoting a sense of sisterhood with other women in the Caribbean, it could help to rally English support for an end to the moral and physical sufferings of the enslaved. Before long, as we shall see, women all over the country were demanding the immediate abolition of slavery, some twenty years after the 1807 parliamentary act to abolish the trade in people to the British Caribbean, an act that, it had been supposed (mistakenly) by some, would result in the natural death of slavery.

The BFS was founded by two local women – Lucy Townsend and Mary Lloyd. Lucy Townsend, an evangelical Anglican who was the daughter of a clergyman and the wife of another, had links with the well-known abolitionist Thomas Clarkson and she asked him for advice in getting involved in the anti-slavery cause. She enlisted the help of Mary Lloyd, a Quaker minister, and together they set up the Society, the first meeting taking place at Lloyd's Birmingham home. The BFS always met at members' homes; this was the early nineteenth century and for 'well-to-do' women to openly meet in a public place was almost unheard of and so their choice of meeting place was restricted by the norms of society. So who were these women? And from what background did they generally come?

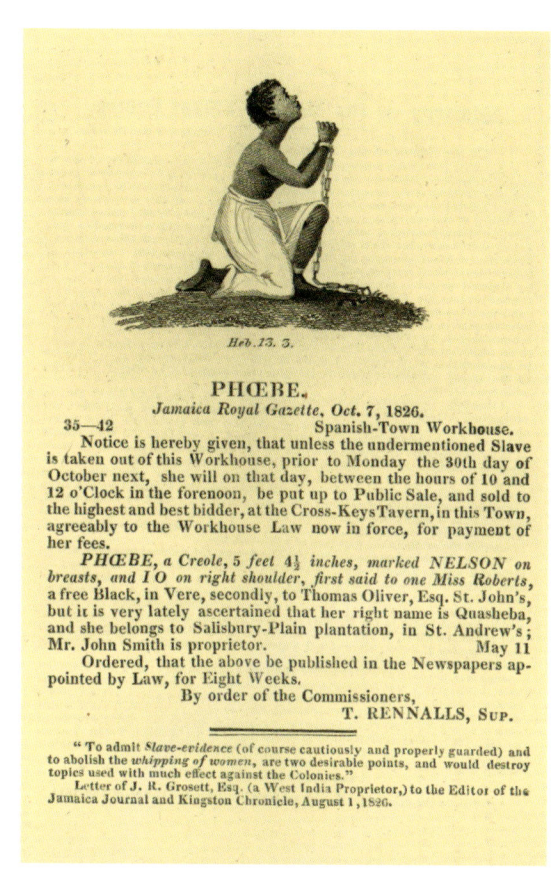

Advert for the sale of Phoebe, a female slave in Jamaica. Jamaica Royal Gazette, Oct. 7, 1826. Courtesy of Birmingham Archives & Heritage.

> '… it appears that in Jamaica, our principle slave Colony, the flogging of females is not abolished, runaway slaves of our own sex, are still identified by their scars, and the recent lacerations of the cart-whip'
>
> BFS 2nd Report, p.118.

SOME MEMBERS OF THE BIRMINGHAM FEMALE SOCIETY

The Society was, in the main, made up of women from wealthy backgrounds, whose key role in life was played out in the domestic arena, raising the children and being a wife, while even those women without families did not usually have to work for a living as they were supported by their fathers and brothers or else were widows of prosperous men. For these reasons, many took up philanthropic work – Mary Lloyd was a member of the Temperance Society and also helped (poor) working-class women and, together with Lucy Townsend, did benevolent works for the Bible Society.

The records of the BFS, held in the Archives at Birmingham Central Library, show the names of women from prominent families in the Midlands – names that many present-day Brummies will have heard of: Wedgewood, Sturge, Cadbury, Lloyd and Galton. Mary-Ann Schimmelpenninck, the daughter of the prominent gun manufacturer, Samuel Galton Jnr., was a member, while Sarah Wedgewood, daughter of the famous potter Josiah, was a district treasurer of the BFS, as was the abolitionist Joseph's sister, Sophia Sturge. It is of note that many of the unmarried women, such as Sophia and Sarah (along with her sister Catherine) had fewer commitments at home and so had more time to devote to the anti-slavery cause.

The BFS did not welcome working-class women into its ranks who, due to high subscription rates, were usually priced out of membership to the Society. According to the Historian Clare Midgley, the Society acted as a kind of social club where middle-class women could mix with ladies similar to themselves while at the same time allowing them to excise philanthropy. Furthermore, she suggests, the lack of interest in working-class women was a sign of the hierarchy so prominent in the England of the day – the middle-classes were the benefactors and the employers while the lower classes were the beneficiaries and the employees. However, those from the lower classes were courted when it came to maximising the signatures on a petition and they were encouraged to join in the abstention from (or boycott of) sugar. The Society also took time to educate all women, regardless of class or status, about slavery and the need to abolish it, but the way this was done varied. When canvassing the poorer areas of Birmingham, the literature used was pitched at a different level than those pamphlets aimed at the middle and upper-classes: today we'd say it was 'dumbed-down' for the masses. In a bid to promote the boycott and the use of sugar made by 'free labour' (East Indian sugar) instead of by slaves, canvassers from the BFS read from a small publication called 'What does your Sugar Cost? A Cottage Conversation on the Subject of British Negro Slavery'. In this way women visited some 80 percent of all Birmingham homes (Sophia Sturge personally knocked on the doors of 3,000 houses in the town!). Pamphlets were also lent out to housewives in the good faith that they would be passed on to neighbours when read. Although not active in the BFS, working-class women signed petitions and supported the boycott in their thousands. The less privileged members of Midlands' society also contributed financially to the BFS, whose third report of 1828 gives details of donations being received from young children, from a 'poor woman' who sold books and pamphlets to neighbours and from a servant in Leicester. This indicates that the BFS did go someway to educating the local population to the plight of the enslaved African, regardless of age or class.

While the Society did seek the co-operation of upper-class women in the boycott, they also targeted them as trend-setters or fashion icons. Rather like the recent tabloid sightings of Keira Knightley parading the streets with one Sainsbury's recyclable 'I'm not a plastic bag', the BLF was eager for high society women being spotted wearing anti-slavery propaganda. Josiah Wedgewood's 'Am I not a Man and a Brother?' cameo, which was commissioned by the Anti-Slavery Society, had already achieved status as a fashion symbol: one which was adopted and adapted by women to read 'Am I not a Woman and a Sister?' The BFS created its own fashion statement in the form of embroidered silk work bags. The bags were made using 'fair-trade' silk (i.e. silk that had not been gathered by enslaved peoples) and were adorned with anti-slavery messages. Inside the bags, the women placed anti-slavery propaganda, including articles from the Jamaica Gazette, which advertised rewards for runaways, and pamphlets written by members of the anti-slavery societies (male and female) in Britain. The workbags were sent to those in prominent positions, including Princess (later, Queen) Victoria, hoping that such women could help publicise their call for the immediate abolition of slavery.

The focus was very much about women helping other women and the plight of the enslaved *Female* became the main occupation of the women of Birmingham.

A SISTERHOOD BASED ON HELPING THE 'HELPLESS'.

We've already established that working-class women living in the same towns and villages as the well-heeled members of these female societies were not, in any way, considered equals to their wealthier and more educated female counterparts. If this was how they perceived their white neighbours, how did the BFS and similar associations view enslaved African women living in the Caribbean?

The general consensus was that they were helpless victims who needed (and no doubt, would appreciate) the financial and moral support of their more fortunate female kind across the Atlantic. For generations, they had been morally and physically degraded and, therefore, African women needed protecting. They were also heathens, and would benefit from religious (Christian) instruction. Time and again examples of the treatment of women in the Caribbean were given in journals such as The Hummingbird, printed and edited in Leicester, and in the societies' annual reports and meetings.

The enslaved Africans were referred to as 'these poor despised outcasts' and the BFS likened 'these oppressed strangers' to 'the oppressed Israelites'. Much was made of the type of punishments unleashed unto the women: in Jamaica, it had been proposed that

Left: Handbag front and back c.1820. Pale blue silk bag with silver clasp, with picture of a Black woman slave with child screen-printed one side, and poem printed on the other side.
© The Religious Society of Friends in Britain.

enslaved women be whipped with a cart-whip instead of a heavier implement known as a cat, and that they should not be indecently exposed while being punished. However, this 'leaner' punishment was rejected. The BFS was outraged and a woman by the name of Charlotte Elizabeth composed a poem, printed in Birmingham, to voice the collective disgust at the treatment of African women.

They also felt responsible for the protection of women and children in the Caribbean who, they felt, were unable to protect themselves. In 1825, £20 was sent to a Female Refuge in Antigua to shelter young women 'the daughters of Negro slaves', whose mothers were unable to 'preserve them from the contagion of ill example', namely prostitutions and promiscuity. Again, the poor 'victims' were unable to help themselves and so, it was considered, it was the place of those in Britain to act as benefactors and to save their bodies and souls. Africans were heathen and so the BFS was keen on supplying the 'spiritual wants of the Negro race'.

Religious schools were set up on various Caribbean islands and money, raised by subscriptions and donations, was sent regularly by the women of Birmingham and the surrounding areas to these places of religious instruction.

How did these views that the enslaved African females were helpless victims tally in the real world? Did the women toiling on the plantations or serving those families that owned or ran them really see themselves as weak insubordinates, reliant on women about whom they know little or nothing? We turn to Mary Prince and her autobiography for some clues to these questions.

MARY PRINCE: HER STORY

Mary Prince was born at Brackish Pond, Bermuda, during the late 1780s. Initially the 'property' of Charles Myners, Mary was sold on time and again, working in turn as a personal slave to a master's daughter, a domestic slave and a field worker. She was sold away from her mother and subject to particularly harsh floggings by one of her mistresses: 'there was no end to my toils, no end to my blows'. Despite attempts to escape, she received such punishments for some five years until she was once again sold on and shipped over to the Turks and Caicos Islands, in her own words 'from one butcher to another'. Her life there improved little: she worked the unforgiving salt ponds for ten years before returning to Bermuda. Her master was unkind to Mary and even to his own daughter – he beat them both, a fate Mary confides that she would have preferred to the job of having to wash him naked in a tub '…my eyes were so full of shame'.

Understandably intolerant of the treatment she received from this master, Mary eventually defended herself after being beaten severely for accidently dropping and smashing some crockery. Her single-mindedness in standing up to a man who would have held physical, economic and even legal power over her, shows Mary's amazing strength and determination. She possessed a sense of what was right, not at all the feeble caricature of African women that the BFS had continually drawn.

Shortly after this episode, in 1818, Mary Prince was sold on to Mr and Mrs Wood for $300 (about £67) and went to live with them in St John's, Antigua, where she worked as nursemaid and washerwoman. Her living conditions were dismal and on top of having to live in an out-house 'swarming with bugs and vermin', she developed

---

Sin first by woman came;- for this
The Lord hath marred her earthly bliss,
    With many a bitter throe;
But mercy tempers wrath, and scorn
Pursues the wretch who add a thorn
    To heaven inflicted woe.

Thine infancy was lulled to rest
On woman's nurturing bosom pressed,
    Enfolded by her arm;
Her hand upheld thy tottering pace:-
And oh! How deep the foul disgrace,
    If thine can work her harm.

Hush not thy nature's conscious plea,
Weak, helpless, succourless, to thee
    Her looks for mercy pray;
He who records each lash, will roll
Torrents of vengeance on they soul!-
Oh! Fling that scourge away

Charlotte Elizabeth

'I defended myself, for I thought it was high time to do so, I then told him I would not live longer with him, for he was a very indecent man – very spiteful, and too indecent; with no shame for his servants, no shame for his own flesh.'

Mary Prince.

rheumatism and had to use a stick to get about. She would have been about 30 years old at this time. Once again she was subject to ill abuse (by both Mr and Mrs Wood), and when she continued to defend herself, voicing to the Mistress her opposition to the injustice of the treatment she received, Mary was beaten. Mary's strength once again shone through. If she could not stop this cruelty through words and reasoning, maybe she could buy her way out of the Woods' household.

Displaying her industriousness, Mary used myriad ways to make money 'for I wanted, by all honest means, to earn money to buy my freedom'. She took in washing and sold produce. Around this time, she began to attend meetings at the Moravian Church, where she learned to read and met a great many people, most of whom were free. One of these was the freeman Daniel Jones, who she married – much to the rage of the Woods. After receiving punishment for her marriage, Mary stood up to Mrs Wood, complaining that she thought such action unfair. The abuse continued and eventually Mary was taken away from her husband to London, where she worked as a servant to the Woods, the couple who had refused to sell her or to let her buy her own freedom.

After a couple of months in London, and thirteen years in the service of the Woods, the physically ill but determined Mary Prince fled the household and sought refuge with the family of Mr Mash, a working man, who, although poor, 'did all that lay in their power to serve me'. She stayed a few months with them until contact with the Anti-Slavery Society led her to service in the home of the abolitionist, Thomas Pringle. It was in his house that Mary Prince wrote her autobiography, *The History of Mary Prince*, one of the first pieces of work by an African woman ever to be published in Britain. Purchasable for as little as 6d., it is a book that, today, gives us an insight into the life of an enslaved African woman both in the Caribbean and in England and, more importantly, it bears testimony to the endurance and fortitude of the African woman, allowing us to challenge the stereotype of her as a weak-willed, helpless and dependent figure. In 1831, Mary's words were used to let people in England know of the realities of slavery in the Caribbean – in this way, Mary Prince played her part in the education of nineteenth century English minds. But to what extent was notice taken of Mary's book and how did the BFS receive her?

'BUT CAN WE TRUST HER?'

The printing of Mary Prince's book, of which three editions were printed in 1831, provoked ill-feeling and libel action. Mr Wood sued the publishers and lost his case. He also attempted to damage Mary's reputation by telling her new abolitionist friends in London that she was ungrateful, worthless and undeserving of sympathy. Although she was considered free whilst in

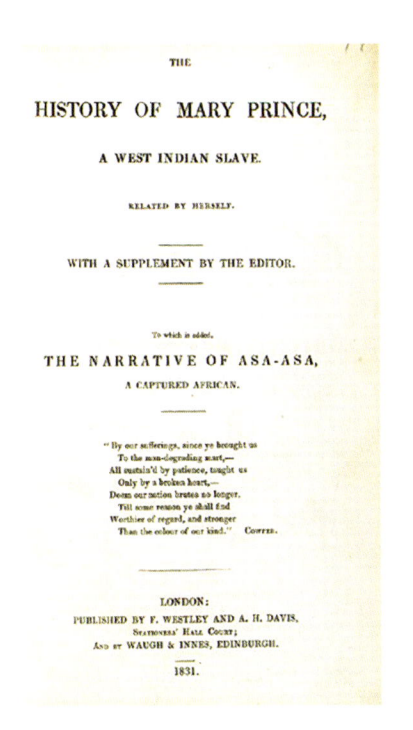

> 'They hire servants in England; and if they don't like them, they send them away: they can't lick them. Let them work ever so hard in England, they are far better off than slaves. If they get a bad master, they give warning and go hire to another. They have their liberty. That's just what we want. We don't mind hard work, if we had proper treatment, and proper wages like English servants, and proper time given in the week to keep us from breaking the Sabbath. But they won't give it: they will have work – work – work, night and day, sick or well, till we are quite done up; and we must not speak up nor look amiss, however much we be abused. And then when we are quite done up, who cares for us, more than for a lame horse? This is slavery. I tell it, to let English people know the truth; and I hope they will never leave off to pray God, and call loud to the great King of England, till all the poor blacks be given free, and slavery done up for evermore.'
>
> **Mary Prince.**

Title page from Mary Prince's autobiography.

> 'In England (Mary) made her election, and quitted my family. This I had no right to object to; and I should have thought no more of it, but not satisfied to leave quietly, she gave every trouble and annoyance in her power, and endeavoured to injure the character of my family by the most vile and infamous falsehoods'.
>
> John A. Wood, 20th October 1830.

> '(Mary) is not, it is true, a very expert housemaid, nor capable of much hard work, (for her constitution appears to be a good deal broken), but she is careful, industrious, and anxious to do her duty and give satisfaction… She possesses considerable natural sense, and has much quickness of observation and discrimination of character. She is remarkable for decency and propriety of conduct – and her delicacy, even in trifling minutiae, has been a trait of special remark by the females of my family.'
>
> Thomas Pringle.

England (under English Law), if she returned to the Caribbean she could be further enslaved – Wood refused to grant her her freedom, to do so might have confirmed his culpability and, he insisted, Mary's book was full of lies. Wood was determined to have his name cleared, and he worked to place doubt in others' minds of the authenticity of Mary's words. His case won the support of two well-known supporters of slavery, MacQueen and Curtin, who slammed Mary's so-called lies in a magazine article in *Blackwood's Magazine*. Mary and the publishers of *History* in turn sued them and won. It is interesting to note that Mary's fight continued even after sharing her experiences on paper; she was called to give evidence at both the trials of her publishers versus Mr Wood and versus the Blackwood's Magazine. The lady was causing quite a stir.

There is no doubt that, at the time of publication, the truths in *History* were questioned, and not only by the likes of Wood and his friends. Mary Prince's words were edited by Pringle's good friend, Susanna Strickland, although, as Thomas Pringle stated in his Preface to her work, it was written in a way that could be understood by the British reader (grammatically) while retaining the original material. In publication, Mary's story was sandwiched by this Preface, a long supplement (also written by the much respected Pringle) and *The Narrative of Louis Asa-Asa: A Captured African*. Pringle and the publishers were well aware that, unused to hearing the words of an African woman, the authenticity of Mary's autobiography would be questioned. And so the pages that surrounded *The History of Mary Prince* were there to lend it credence – the word of the enslaved African, after all, was not nearly as valuable as that of the free white person. By 1831, it had been so for far too long for attitudes to change with the release of one of the few books written by an African ever to have reached the hands of the British public. And so, Mary needed validation.

The Birmingham Female Society sought such validation through correspondence with Thomas Pringle and his family; the word of such a respected family in London had more clout than that of an African woman who had been in the country just three years. The BFS sent regular contributions to the London Anti-Slavery Society, of which Pringle was Secretary (in 1830, he sent a letter to thank the women for a donation of £50, for example) – they were on good terms with him, they trusted him. At a meeting held at Mrs Moilliet's house in Handsworth (daughter of chemist and Tipton soap factory, James Keir), a letter, signed 'Yours very truly, (Mrs) M. Pringle' and addressed to Mrs Townsend of West-Bromwich, was read out to the members. That letter confirmed that 'marks of severe punishment' on Mary's body had been witnessed by her very own eyes. Therefore, Mary's story must be believed – she had suffered cruelty indeed. Mrs Pringle's testimony was 'corroborated' by Susanna Strickland, Mrs Pringle's sister Susan Brown and her friend Martha Browne, adding necessary weight to the evidence. Happy with such proof, the members of the BFS agreed to forward £5 to Mary's fund. They also sent £5 to the widow and child of Ashton Warner, a formerly enslaved African born in St Vincent, who had made his own way to England and whose Narrative had also been edited by Strickland. A letter of thanks received from Thomas Pringle in April 1834 shows that the Society had donated a further £70 to the Anti-Slavery Society in London.

We know from a postscript by Pringle in the second edition of *The History of Mary Prince* that our heroine's health had further deteriorated and that she was losing her sight. However, after the trails of 1833, we lose all contact with this remarkable woman who lived to tell her story in an age when slavery was still common-place in the British West Indies.

CONCLUSION

It is apparent from Mary's story and the suspicion surrounding her that African women were seen in no way to be the equals of women belonging to the BFS. Despite their calls for sisterhood, these white middle-class women, did not have the skills necessary to break the barriers that were such a large part of the patriarchal and hierarchical society in which they survived. They had their own roles in society, subordinate to men, and it followed that those less privileged (and less formally educated) than themselves should be their subordinates. The refusal to accept working women in Britain as equals was just part of that structure and so it should come as no surprise that African women, who resided even further down the social scale, should be helped from afar and not necessarily as individuals.

The BFS, and the many such societies that sprang up in its image, was a safe place for women of a certain class to meet and to feel that they were doing good, that they were helping others. Their sources were periodicals such as the *Jamaica Gazette* and essays or pamphlets written by male abolitionists in Britain. There were few, if any, first-hand accounts of the lives of enslaved women that members of the BFS could turn to. And so, they were portrayed as defenceless dependents. However, by denying African women a sense of ownership, by treating them as the victims who were unable to fend for themselves, white middle-class women did not succeed in promoting sisterhood (indeed they had probably never intended to). What The Female Society for the Relief of British Negro Slaves did achieve, however, was to awaken people in Britain to the cruel conditions in which millions had lived and continued to live. In this way, it may have furthered the abolitionist cause. It was up to the few voices that reached British shores, like that of Mary Prince, to help tell the whole story.

'My husband having read to me the passage in your last letter to him, expressing a desire to be furnished with some description of the marks of former ill-usage on Mary Prince's person, - I beg in reply to state, that the whole of the back part of her body is distinctly scarred, and, as it were chequered, with the vestiges of severe floggings…. Mary affirms, that all these scars were occasioned by the various cruel punishments she has mentioned or referred to in her narrative; and of the entire truth of this statement I have no hesitation in declaring myself perfectly satisfied…'

M. Pringle to Mrs Townsend, 28th March 1831.

11

Black Antislavery Narratives and Transatlantic Identities in Birmingham

Dr Andy Green

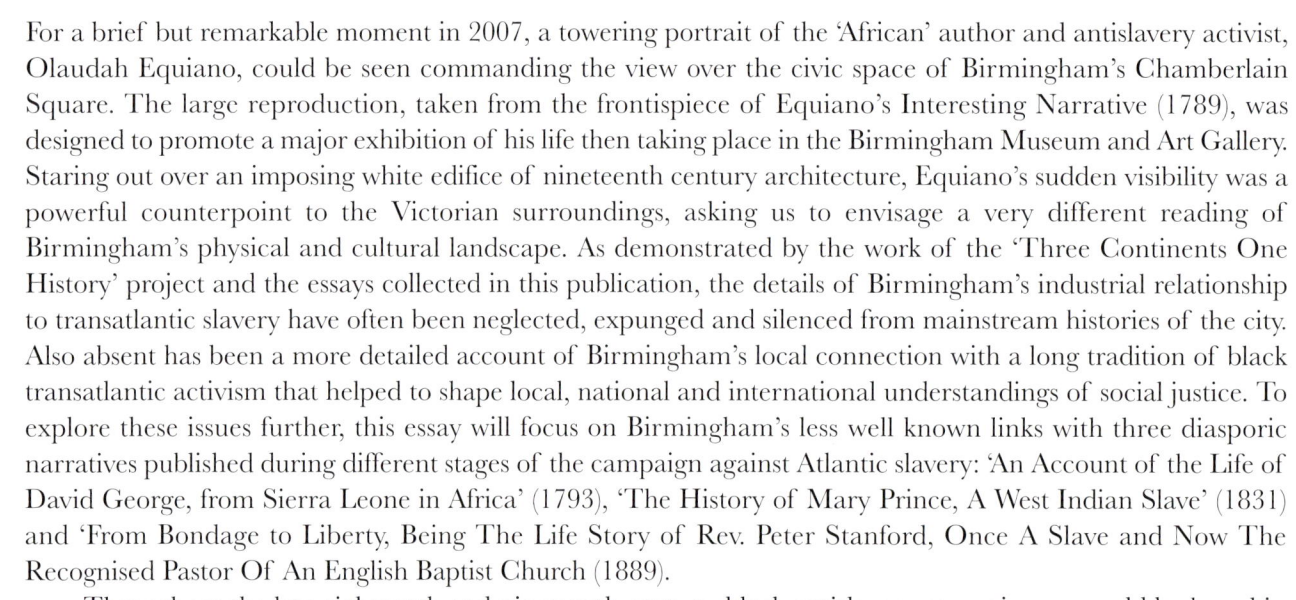

For a brief but remarkable moment in 2007, a towering portrait of the 'African' author and antislavery activist, Olaudah Equiano, could be seen commanding the view over the civic space of Birmingham's Chamberlain Square. The large reproduction, taken from the frontispiece of Equiano's Interesting Narrative (1789), was designed to promote a major exhibition of his life then taking place in the Birmingham Museum and Art Gallery. Staring out over an imposing white edifice of nineteenth century architecture, Equiano's sudden visibility was a powerful counterpoint to the Victorian surroundings, asking us to envisage a very different reading of Birmingham's physical and cultural landscape. As demonstrated by the work of the 'Three Continents One History' project and the essays collected in this publication, the details of Birmingham's industrial relationship to transatlantic slavery have often been neglected, expunged and silenced from mainstream histories of the city. Also absent has been a more detailed account of Birmingham's local connection with a long tradition of black transatlantic activism that helped to shape local, national and international understandings of social justice. To explore these issues further, this essay will focus on Birmingham's less well known links with three diasporic narratives published during different stages of the campaign against Atlantic slavery: 'An Account of the Life of David George, from Sierra Leone in Africa' (1793), 'The History of Mary Prince, A West Indian Slave' (1831) and 'From Bondage to Liberty, Being The Life Story of Rev. Peter Stanford, Once A Slave and Now The Recognised Pastor Of An English Baptist Church (1889).

Throughout the late eighteenth and nineteenth century, black antislavery campaigners would be heard in political gatherings, non-conformist church halls and meeting rooms across Britain. Following in Equiano's footsteps, other social commentators such as Frederick Douglass would make their own personal visits to Birmingham in order to agitate, read extracts from their work, and distribute publications. In doing so, they engaged with but also challenged the leadership of local antislavery circles by dramatically articulating their own personal struggles for social freedom and calling for an end to the devastating ongoing trade in 'human cargoes'. In exceptional cases, evidence from local archives suggests that one or two of these activists even decided to make

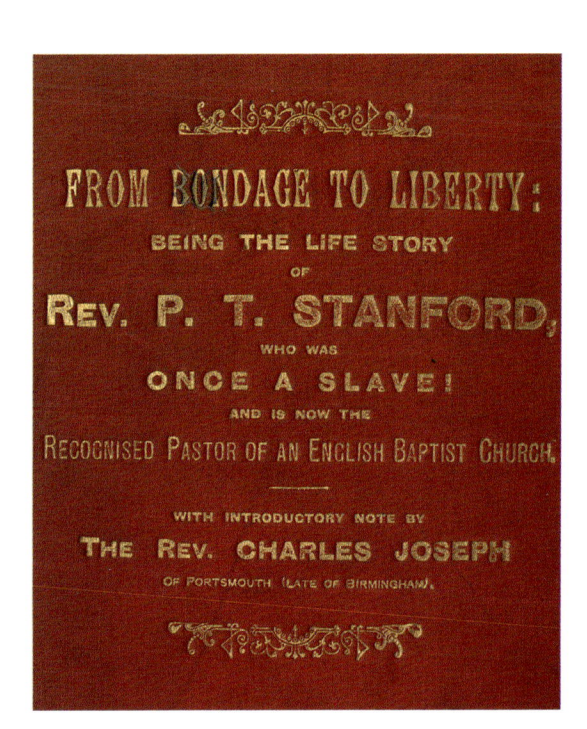

Title page of Rev. Stanford's autobiography. Courtesy of Birmingham Archives & Heritage.

Birmingham a more settled, if not permanent, home. The Narrative of the Life of James Watkins (1853) tells us how its author had escaped from slavery in Maryland and fled to England to find a new home of freedom. 'In closing my account of Birmingham', Watkins writes, 'I must again say that I have found more heartiness in their sympathy- more earnestness in their desire to forward my interests, and more friendliness at their firesides than in any town I have seen'. Yet such impressions of Birmingham must be treated with caution: other migrants encountered a less benign side of 'polite' society. Rev. Peter Stanford's contribution to the civic and religious life of Birmingham as a black Baptist minister in the late nineteenth century prompted a volatile response of admiration and racially charged hostility from local commentators and citizens.

Autobiographical writings by previously enslaved men and women who emancipated themselves from the brutal horrors of plantation life represent a vital form of social resistance. While slaveholders enforced the scientific and cultural dehumanisation of Africans, authorship offered ways for some of those who escaped bondage to attack white racist societies, reclaiming agency, identity and history. Publications of first hand insights into slavery were highly prized by local and national abolitionist organisations, religious groups and missionary societies who believed they needed to show direct proof of the injustices taking place. Yet because of the white liberal agenda within which black literary voices became enfolded, relationships between black antislavery authors and white humanitarian circles could themselves become highly problematic. Experiences of the transatlantic trade told in person or in print by black abolitionists often highlighted a struggle pitted not only against the barbaric practises of white slaveholders but also the equally ingrained cultural assumptions of white abolitionists whose names have dominated our understanding of emancipation.

Uneasy debates surrounding the need for black literature to give, above all, a 'true' and 'authentic' picture of slavery have lasted until the present day, as can be seen at the heart of recent arguments over Equiano's identity and place of birth. Following Vincent Caretta's persuasive argument that Equiano may have been born in South Carolina, opinion has been divided as to why the author subsequently chose to label himself an 'African'. In cases such as these, the historian's task is not always to find a definitive answer, but to explore the full range of questions connected to the unfolding evidence. The narratives addressed in this essay show how black authors were interested not only in reporting the brute 'facts' of slavery, but also aimed at creating confrontational political protest through a series of shifting identities and sophisticated literary effects that could manipulate the presumptions of a white audience. In this context, Equiano's letter to Birmingham Aris's Gazette in 1790 holds the potential to be read in a far more subversive and ironic light than we might first imagine.

THE 'AFRICAN' DAVID GEORGE AND THE 'SERAPHIC' SAMUEL PEARCE

Adding new questions to these debates and unexpectedly drawing Birmingham further into the complex relationship between black identity and authorship, the Baptist Annual Register of 1793 shows that Equiano's autobiography was not the only example of an eighteenth century 'African' narrative connected with the industrial heartland of Britain. Contained in this issue is an entry whose full title holds a local twist: 'An Account Of The

---

'I beg you to suffer me thus publicly to express my grateful acknowledgements for their Favours and for the fellow-feeling they have discovered for my very poor and much oppressed countrymen; these Acts of Kindness and Hospitality have filled me with a longing desire to see these worthy Friends on my own estate in Africa, when the richest Produce of it should be devoted to their Entertainment; they should there partake of the luxuriant Pine-apples and the well-flavoured virgin Palm Wine, and to heighten the Bliss, I would burn a certain kind of Tree, that would afford us Light as clear and brilliant as the Virtues of my Guests. I am Sir, your humble Servant, GUSTAVAS VASA, the African'.

(Birmingham Aris's Gazette, June 19th, 1790).

(473)

An Account of the Life of Mr. DAVID GEORGE, from Sierra Leone in Africa; given by himself in a Conversation with Brother RIPPON of London, and Brother PEARCE of Birmingham.

I was born in Essex county, Virginia, about 50 or 60 miles from Williamsburg, on Nottaway river, of parents who were brought from Africa, but who had not the fear of God before their eyes. The first work I did was fetching water, and carding of cotton; afterwards I was sent into the field to work about the Indian corn and tobacco, till I was about 19 years old. My father's name was John, and my mother's Judith. I had four brothers, and four sisters, who, with myself, were all born in slavery: our master's name was Chapel—a very bad man to the Negroes. My oldest sister was called Patty; I have seen her several times so whipped that her back has been all corruption, as though it would rot. My brother Dick ran away, but they caught him, and brought him home; and as they were going to tie him up, he broke away again, and they hunted him with horses and dogs, till they took him; then they hung him up to a cherry-tree in the yard, by his two hands, quite naked, except his breeches, with his feet about half a yard from the ground. They tied his legs close together, and put a pole between them, at one end of which one of the owner's sons sat, to keep him down, and another son at the other. After he had received 500 lashes, or more, they washed his back with salt water, and whipped it in, as well as rubbed it in with a rag; and then directly sent him to work in pulling off the suckers of tobacco. I also have been whipped many a time on my naked skin, and sometimes till the blood has run down over my waistband; but the greatest grief I then had was to see them whip my mother, and to hear her, on her knees, begging for mercy. She was master's cook, and if they only thought she might do any thing better than she did, instead of speaking to her as to a servant, they would strip her directly, and cut away. I believe she was on her death-bed when I got off, but I have never heard since. Master's rough and cruel usage was the reason of my running-away. Before this time I used to drink, but not steal; did not fear hell, was without knowledge; though I went sometimes to Nottaway, the English church, about eight or nine miles off. I left the plantation about midnight, walked all night, got into Brunswick county, then over Roanoak river, and soon met with some White travelling people, who helped me

Hh 3 on

Baptist Annual Register, 1793. Courtesy of Birmingham Archives & Heritage.

Life of David George from Sierra Leone in Africa Given by Himself in Conversation with Brother Rippon of London and Brother Pearce of Birmingham'. The 'Brother Pearce' in question was a young and spiritually zealous Baptist minister imbued with a desire to spread Christian values across the globe. Originally born in the slave-trading port of Bristol, Pearce came to Birmingham in 1790 to take up the ministry of the Canon Street Baptist Church, where his local reputation for spiritual intensity would strongly increase the numbers of the congregation and eventually earn him the name of the 'seraphic'. A growing evangelical belief also led Pearce to become a founder member of the Baptist Missionary Society in 1792. Set within this context of local, national and international aspirations, the significance of the connection with David George's Account is heightened by the fact that Pearce's name can also be found on the subscriber list to Equiano's narrative of 1790. Three years later, it seems, the same minister from Birmingham's Canon Street Baptist Church was to become involved once more in the publication of a black narrative outlining the horrors of transatlantic slavery, from what the title implied was an 'authentic' African perspective.

Ostensibly facilitated by Samuel Pearce, the 'Account' by David George encompasses a complex map of changing geographies and a criss-crossing range of debates over race, religion and national identity. Originally born into slavery in Virginia, the defeat of the British at the end of the American revolution allowed George to travel as a free 'black loyalist' to Nova Scotia, where he first began to practice his Baptist faith as a preacher for the local black community. However, the hostility he faced from members of the white congregation became a factor in his decision to make the journey with other members of his church to play a role in founding the Sierra Leone settlement in 1792. Subtly echoing aspects of Equiano's frontispiece description, this is the 'African' setting that George highlights in the title of his own autobiographical sketch. Originally born to African parents, George's memories of his birthplace in the United States are framed only by abuse and mistreatment, captured for the reader in a language that is both chillingly direct, as well as emotionally and physically visceral.

Explicit images of physical torture in first-hand antislavery accounts have long been seen as playing into and constructing white social attitudes of patriarchal sympathy. George's description of his mother on her knees mirrors the imagined plight of the famous antislavery medallion 'Am I Not A Man and A Brother', itself an artefact which had its origins in West Midlands intellectual circles, created by Josiah Wedgewood in 1787. Yet whilst George's narrative uses such scenes to engender sympathy for those who suffered under slavery, the wider structure of his text can be seen to portray a subtly different image. Despite the image of black subjugation we are shown in the opening scene, the overall impact of George's story draws power from its incredible geographical sweep as his story criss-crosses national boundaries, journeying across the American South, Canada, Sierra Leone, Britain, and, we might finally argue, Birmingham itself, summoned in the last word of George's title. Embarking on these journeys, the narrator of this account is someone who responds to and challenges his circumstances, rather than merely being a disempowered or abject 'slave'. Was this nation-traversing story sent to Pearce as part of a letter by George from Sierra Leone? Or did the author of the account go so far as to visit Birmingham when he visited Britain in 1793? Unfortunately, there are currently no records to show where or when David George gave his story to Brother Rippon and Brother Pearce, facilitated through their contacts with the Baptist Missionary Society. We can only speculate whether George visited the original Canon Street Baptist church, which in its original site lay in close proximity to St Philips churchyard.

If a personal encounter between the two men did take place, it seems unlikely that the 'Brother Pearce' of Birmingham would have regarded George as a social equal. Instead, the account Pearce took down would have been understood as an important symbol of the power of the Baptist religion to lift up those of a 'lower' order into a more civilised Christian class. Either way, what can be seen as George's extended links with one of Birmingham's leading and influential non-conformist churches suggests his entry in the Baptist Annual Register may well have been picked up by other citizens of Birmingham, including local intellectuals and businessmen such as Matthew Boulton and James Watt who themselves had more than a passing interest in the development of the settlement in Sierra Leone. Playing a role in the production of this crucial piece of early antislavery literature, the story of David George's connection with Samuel Pearce highlights for us a shifting set of identities and locations that draw late eighteenth century Birmingham into a range of abolitionist contexts. Yet, whilst Pearce's legacy after his death was to be illuminated as one of Canon Street's 'divinely' inspired founding fathers, any memory of Birmingham's connection to David George was to fall into obscurity and shadow.

> 'I also have been whipped many a time on my naked skin and sometimes till the blood has run down over my waistband, but the greatest grief I then had was to see them whip my mother, and to hear her on her knees, begging for mercy. She was master's cook, and if they only thought she might do anything better than she did, instead of speaking to her as to a servant, they would strip her directly and cut away. I believe she was on her deathbed when I got off, but I have never heard since'.
>
> (An Account Of The Life of David George from Sierra Leone in Africa Given by Himself in Conversation with Brother Rippon of London and Brother Pearce of Birmingham, 1793).

'THE HISTORY OF MARY PRINCE' AND 'THE FEMALE SOCIETY FOR BIRMINGHAM FOR THE RELIEF OF BRITISH NEGRO SLAVES'

Overlapping voices, conflicting cultural memories and historical signs are stored and layered throughout Birmingham's restless landscape, its streets shaped and reshaped by histories of constant migration, its public spaces deeply entangled with debates over liberty, faith, freedom, business, culture and identity. In the very places we take most for granted, important stories lie buried that once played an important role in the history of the city. Standing by an overlooked corner of St. Philips' Cathedral churchyard in a position facing outwards onto the corner of Temple Row West, a large gravestone can be seen inscribed with the name 'Samuel Lines. Artist'. The 'Lines' in question here was a significant figure of Birmingham's growing artistic societies, a drawing master who became one of the founding fathers of the Royal Birmingham Society of Artists. It is a gravestone which communicates something to us about the way in which a town renowned as a place of work, labour and industry was becoming ever more interested in art, craft and culture. Surprisingly, the same fading inscription can also be shown to reveal a number of connections to early nineteenth century antislavery activism in the area. With absolutely no visible relationship between Samuel Lines' gravestone and Birmingham's history as an important location of antislavery campaigning, it is only through a study of the city's profoundly important archive collections that an underlying set of connections becomes apparent, linking this public space with local women's abolitionist circles and the publication of 'The History of Mary Prince' (1831).

Women's antislavery culture had one of its first strongholds in Birmingham. Driven by a strong contingent of powerful non-conformist Quaker families such as the Sturges and the Cadburys, The Female Society for

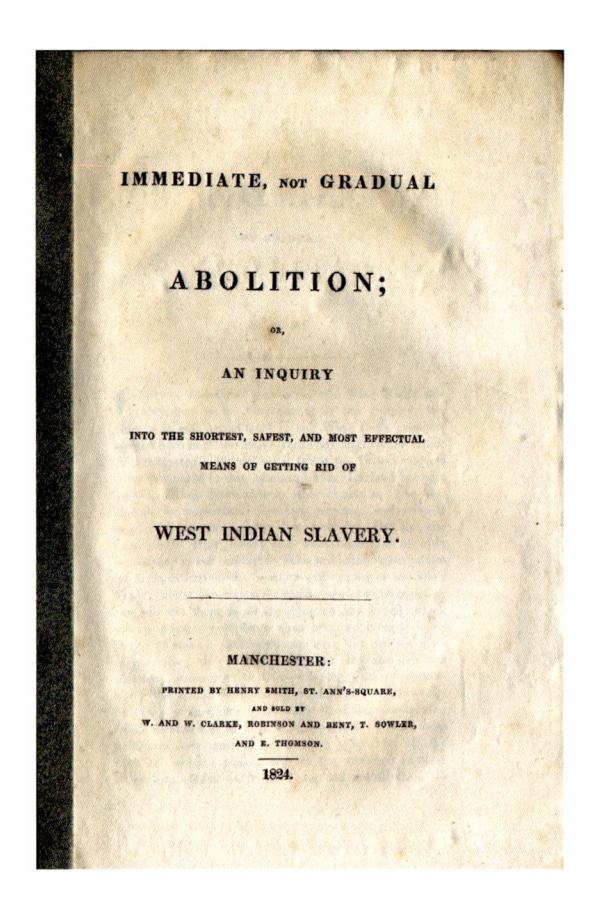

Title page of Elizabeth Heyrick's pamphlet on immediate, not gradual abolition. © The Religious Society of Friends in Britain.

Birmingham, West Bromwich, Wednesbury, Walsall, and their Respective Neighbourhoods, for the Relief of British Negro Slaves was officially founded in 1825 by Lucy Townsend and Mary Lloyd. Through a range of activities and tactics, the women who were part of this society called for an 'immediate' and not 'gradual' end to all ongoing forms of slavery, powerfully promoting boycotts on the use of slave grown sugar. One way in which the campaign group raised money for its antislavery causes involved producing vividly illustrated antislavery 'albums', which became circulated across an overlapping network of those interested in reforming conditions in the West Indies. Donations gathered from the production of these illustrated albums allowed the local society to economically support individual cases of cruel mistreatment on the plantation. The women's crucial decision to employ illustrated antislavery propaganda meant that the society also had the potential to educate the large proportion of the illiterate working classes in Birmingham about West Indian slavery, drawing on emotive imagery of a transatlantic sisterhood to spur British women to come to the aid of the enslaved African in the Caribbean.

However, whilst the women self-reliantly created their own antislavery textiles and busily organised local and national petitions, the production of their album artefacts required extra contributions from artists who could be trusted for their sympathy towards the female abolitionist cause. Digging into the collection of records preserved by the Female Society for Birmingham, we discover how it was none other than 'Samuel Lines' who was responsible for providing the startlingly iconic images that can be found throughout the society's albums. Bringing his name to life for us with a human touch, the minutes of a meeting on 13th of April 1826 reveal to us Samuel Lines' antislavery sympathies by reporting how he had given his time and efforts as an illustrator free of charge to the society. Meanwhile, as evidence connecting these albums with the production of important transatlantic narratives, the same women's minute book later tells us that a portion of money raised by the society was being donated to a Caribbean woman who would soon become famous: 'That five pounds be appropriated' states an entry dated April 1831, 'by this society to originate a Fund for the support of Mary Prince'.

These underlying relationships give Birmingham a fascinating and unexpected place in the chain of events surrounding the publication of The History of Mary Prince. Contained within this powerful and famous work, Mary Prince's often quoted description of the 'horrors of slavery' would have been read as a rallying call for the ongoing work of female antislavery societies in Birmingham, particularly as it culminates in what appears to be a traditional appeal to the British to 'break the chains'. Yet such statements should not be taken to imply her sense of deferral to the authority of white abolitionists. Certainly, Prince's story was carefully structured by those who sought to tell an 'appropriate' story of her past, Susanna Strickland and Thomas Pringle of the national Anti Slavery Society. In the face of these restrictions, her voice manages to retain a subversive force, defiantly attacking slavery and questioning global imbalances of power. Instead of encountering a work which was subservient to British middle class perspectives, early audiences would find themselves confronted by a narrator who was not afraid to challenge their authority: 'I have been a slave... I have felt what a slave feels... I would have all the good people in England know it too'.

Prince's constant and uncompromising stress upon the word 'I' during the construction of her famous antislavery polemic retains its power for us today. Her set of personal declarations serve as a dramatic verbal tool that underline the agency and authority of Mary Prince as an author. In a voice which refutes her body's status as an 'object' under the yoke of slavery, Prince's declaration that she has 'felt what a slave feels' encourages us to look beyond the page and remember the anonymous struggles of those women who fought against their status as 'chattel'. Perhaps, therefore, rather than asking what status Mary Prince would have had without the Birmingham women, we should also ask ourselves the reverse question – what goal or understanding of slavery could these radical middle class women from nineteenth century Birmingham have had without rebels like Mary Prince? Whilst it may have been economic capital that Birmingham women supplied to Mary Prince, it was an equally important 'moral' capital and agenda that Prince returned to the female antislavery activists of Birmingham.

In whichever way we view the relationship, it seems incredible that the history of women's activism in Birmingham remains so undervalued when it can claim such powerful transatlantic precedents. Today, The History of Mary Prince remains more vital than ever as the first female-centred narrative depicting the experiences of an African woman in Caribbean plantation slavery. Whether or not Prince visited the West Midlands in person, we know for certain that her 'voice' was heard here, spreading an influence over events unfolding across the Atlantic. From a local gravestone, to some records in the city archives, we find an unexpected chain of connections leading us from Birmingham today to a Caribbean context of resistance.

BIRMINGHAM'S BLACK MINSTER: REV. PETER STANFORD AND HOPE STREET CHAPEL

With constant mutinies and rebellions confronting European plantation owners, slave narratives such as The History of Mary Prince undoubtedly also played a part in events leading to the West Indies Emancipation Act in 1833 and the subsequent end of the corrupt 'Apprenticeship' system which perpetuated inequalities until 1838. After this date, many antislavery societies now turned their attention to countries where the 'evils' of slavery continued unchecked and unabated. This shift of focus ensured that communications between Birmingham and a range of black authors and activists continued on into the late nineteenth century. In America, worsening conditions for plantation slaves in the south culminated with the passing of the Fugitive Slave Law in 1850. With nowhere remaining safe for an escaped slave, Britain was now increasingly visited by African Americans seeking their liberation. Travelling up and down the country as campaigning activists and authors, they protested the decree which meant any escaped slave in the north United States could be legally returned to shackles in the south. These diasporic British-American relations formed the unsteady political context which eventually led to the arrival into Birmingham of Peter Stanford in 1887, another figure who embodies the telling evidence of a powerful pre-twentieth century black presence in the migratory contexts of the West Midlands.

The growing range of black activists we currently know to have visited Birmingham after 1850 include authors, poets and orators such as James Watkins, J.W.C Pennington, Alexander Crummell, Samuel Ringgold Ward, Amanda Smith, Ida B. Wells, Highland Henry Garnet, Booker T. Washington and Rev. Peter Stanford.

'That the thanks of this meeting are also presented to S. Lines, who has readily and with utmost kindness executed all the drawings for this Society, without receiving any remunerations for efforts which without his aid, must have cost this society a larger sum and have prevented some of its exertions for the relief of Negro Slaves'.

(Minute Book of the Birmingham Female Society for the Relief of the British Negro Slave, 13th April, 1826).

'Oh the horrors of slavery! How the thought of it pains my heart! But the truth ought to be told of it; and what my eyes have seen I think it is my duty to relate; for few people in England knows what slavery is. I have been a slave- I have felt what a slave feels, and I know what a slave knows; and I would have all the good people in England know it too, that they may break our chains, and set us free.'

(The History of Mary Prince, 1831).

> 'I was born into slavery, and inherited the misery and suffering inseparable from that accursed institution. The date even of my birth was shrouded in obscurity, and it was only by subsequent enquiry that I ascertained, on the best available authority, that I was born on the 21st February, 1859, at Hampton, Virginia, United States of America'.
>
> **(From Bondage to Liberty: Being the Life Story of the Rev. Peter Stanford Who Was Once a Slave And Is Now the Recognised Pastor of an English Baptist Church, 1889).**

> 'And today, not withstanding my birth as a slave and the colour of my skin, I am pastor in this great city of Birmingham. I have been libelled, slandered, ostracised, suspected, and opposed; but in all these troubles I have not lacked many true Christian friends'.
>
> **(From Bondage to Liberty: Being the Life Story of the Rev. Peter Stanford Who Was Once a Slave And Is Now the Recognised Pastor of an English Baptist Church, 1889).**

Despite what had become a misleading association with Britain as a 'land of freedom' for the exiled slave, these black transatlantic abolitionists often arrived to face hostility, disbelief and racism. White liberals who offered to support these African American authors undoubtedly continued to imagine themselves, barring one or two exceptions, as occupying a more sophisticated cultural position than the visiting 'ex-slave'. Civic societies promoted an understanding of freedom in which white Christian culture remained the philanthropic benevolent force that guided black peoples into a 'proper' understanding of emancipation. This can be seen most vividly in the case of Peter Stanford, a larger than life figure who brought the fight for racial justice to Birmingham's doorstep, more than one hundred years after Equiano had been the first black author to visit the area.

Whilst an African Caribbean migrant named George Cousins is known to have been employed as a Baptist minister in the Cradley Heath area in the 1830s, it was Rev. Peter Stanford who worked as the first black minister for inner Birmingham. Much of the information we have about Stanford's life comes from his astonishing autobiographical work, 'From Bondage to Liberty' written and published while he was living in the city. Born into slavery on the 21st February 1859 in Hampton, Virginia, Stanford was just two years old when the Civil War broke out in America. His long subsequent series of struggles and adventures even include being kidnapped by a group of Native Americans who teach the young Stanford to hunt and fish. After a later conversion to the Baptist faith and spending time in New York, Stanford travelled to England in 1883 to work as a 'mendicant missionary', visiting Liverpool, London and Bradford and finally Birmingham in 1887. Two years later, Hope Street Baptist Church in Highgate would ask Stanford to become the local pastor on May 8th 1889.

If Stanford had the support of a number of important co-religionists such as Charles Vince, he did not become smoothly 'assimilated' into broader religious civic society. Before taking up the position offered at Hope Street Baptist Church, the African American seems to have become embroiled in what appears to be a shadowy battle with some unnamed yet powerful critics who apparently regard him as either a 'fraud' or incapable of fulfilling the duties of a Baptist minister. Racial tensions appear to hang over this chapter of Stanford life, of which the full details are not yet known. Overcoming this struggle for local recognition, Stanford began to serve the Highgate mission and married a local woman who helped him with his ministry, thereby making the history of mixed race marriages in Birmingham a further part of his dramatic story. Whatever his problems with some Baptist ministers, it would seem that Stanford's popularity with the white working-class congregation must have grown rapidly. From Bondage to Liberty states that its author is 'contemplating the building here, in Birmingham, of a Wilberforce Memorial Church'. It is perhaps to this local Highgate community that we can attribute Stanford's later statement that 'leaving my Birmingham church was the greatest trial of my life'.

There is currently little evidence to say what became of Stanford's idea for a 'Wilberforce Memorial Church' in Birmingham. Nevertheless, fragmentary insights surrounding Stanford's relationship to the city suggests a figure of considerable social prominence that some conservative Baptists and leading citizens may have perceived as threatening or unwanted. The title of Stanford's autobiography, From Bondage to Liberty, itself claims radical political agency by self consciously echoing a long tradition of black antislavery narratives. More specifically, its title plays on one of the most famous slave narratives of the mid-nineteenth century, Frederick Douglass's My Bondage And My Freedom (1855). Stanford would have been aware that Douglass, Equiano and many other black abolitionists had visited Birmingham before him and would have seen himself as part of this transatlantic tradition of radical black resistance. Following his return to the United States in 1895 to campaign against the ongoing of practice of Southern lynching, one of Stanford's other literary achievements was to write a history of black activism entitled The Tragedy of The Negro In America (1897).

In Birmingham today, there is no plaque or physical reminder of Stanford's important legacy. Only a small number of published descriptions of him are currently to be found in the city's archive collections. Notably, a late nineteenth century volume entitled Birmingham Faces and Place VI, includes Stanford as one of the rare, if not the only, examples of a black civic personage in its pages. Its brief portrait of Stanford highlights the deeply problematic racial attitudes of some white middle class citizens who would have been able to purchase the book. The anonymous author of Stanford's description in Faces and Places foregrounds his subject as a 'social curiosity', raising explicitly racist ideas concerning Stanford skin colour. More subtly, by emphasising the ministers capacity for 'singing', 'raciness' and 'weed smoking', the distorted portrait of Stanford also tacitly conforms to minstrelsy stereotypes made acceptable as entertainment through the performance of American acts touring throughout Britain in the nineteenth century. Despite all these hostile racial assumptions, or more likely because of them, an image of Stanford emerges which reflects on his powerful desire to 'kick against patronage' as Birmingham's first black pastor. But it was most likely to have been Stanford's support from working class people, rather than the bourgeois elite, that allowed him to do so.

Contesting the representation given in Faces and Places, Stanford's own words in From Bondage to Liberty attest to a social and literary agency which can be situated within a long history of transatlantic authorship and activism. Entangled in the legacy of Birmingham's civic development, yet marginalised from its history books, Stanford's life reminds us once more how the physical space which surrounds our everyday life can be surprisingly linked to untold histories that have gone before. Few today would expect the current Highgate Baptist Church to stand guard over such an important set of international histories – a fact of which Rev. Paul Walker, its current minister and leading Stanford scholar, is only too aware. Linking us to this forgotten past, the writings by activists such as Mary Prince, David George and Rev. Peter Stanford need to be remembered and celebrated as part of a local history rooted in diaspora and political debate. To avoid treating their life stories in ways that might evoke a sentimental multicultural fantasy of 'abolition', we should engage with their narratives in ways that complicate our notion of how Birmingham debated slavery through many different voices and conflicting social, political and racial agendas.

By uncovering these vital alternative histories we reinvest our landscape with new meaning. Rev. Peter Stanford's legacy was to defiantly challenge the civic ideals of progress and racial superiority by speaking out and arguing that we should not let the injustices of the past be silenced beneath a veneer of 'forward' progress. It is a legacy that needs to be better remembered.

'Loss of life by unauthorized violence, and the resulting unhappiness to others, is called a tragedy; and, every tragedy of real life has stimulated the best and the worst passions of mankind to vigorous interest and exertion. All tragedies, however, have not been caused by unauthorized violence; the pages of history are black with records of the foulest crimes, of violations of human rights and divine law, by violence authorized and made legal by men in whom power was vested.'

(The Tragedy of the Negro in America, 1897).

'Those who have never seen Mr Stanford in the flesh (and there must be few in Birmingham), and who have preconceived notions as to the black ness of all "niggers," would be surprised to know that though "coloured," Mr Stanford is by no means as "black" as he might be imagined to be […] He is, too, a living example of what the much despised negro can be made by the influence of education, refinement and culture[…] He is, he tells us, inclined to "kick" against patronage, and believing in the equality of men, prefers to stand on his own merits than to cling to the coat tails of any one […] Outside his ministerial duties Mr Stanford takes a lively interest in political and social matters. He is a member of three or four of the Birmingham Friendly Societies, and takes a great interest in social and philanthropic work, has a cheerful racy style of speaking, is an ardent teetotaller but lover of fragrant weed. He is a first rate singer and musician, and does much in this way to brighten up the services at his pretty little church, where he appears to be doing a good work.'

(Birmingham Faces and Places VI ,1894)

Acknowledgements

On a complex project of this nature which has run for fifteen months, there are a number of individuals and organisations that we would like to thank publicly for the contributions that they have made in enabling us to meet our varied objectives and outputs. At the beginning, it was the assistance of individuals such as Guy Collier, Martin Blissett and Judy Smith which helped to ensure that a distinctive project, worthy of the aspirations of our community, could be successfully put together.

As the project entered its research phase, other individuals and organisations contributed. We would like to thank the following for their assistance rendered to the research process: Stephanie Bennett, of Royal Regiment of Fusiliers Museum, Warwick, Colonel John Lowles, of Norton Barracks, Worcester and Willie Turner, of Staffordshire Regiment Museum for sharing their expert knowledge on the 6th, 29th and 64th Regiments of Foot, respectively; Mark Hailstone for allowing us to consult his undergraduate dissertation on women abolitionists in Birmingham; Gay Lawrence, Colton House, Colton, for sharing her knowledge of and personal records on the Burt Family; Dr Malcolm Dick, University of Birmingham, for answering many research questions; John Ellis for posting copies of his own work into Black Drummers of the 29th Regiment; and Graeme Clarke, of Dr Johnson's Birthplace, Lichfield, for information on Francis Barber. For the help offered in unearthing the links between Birmingham and the European Slave Trade, we would like to extend a general thanks to the following: staff at Birmingham Archives and Heritage Service (Birmingham Central Library); staff at Warwick, Stafford and Leicester Records' Offices; and staff at the National Archives, Kew.

The project has been the beneficiary of a range of volunteer support. Three Continents, One History would like to give special thanks to Dunya Mahachi, LJ and Ras Tread for delivering some informative and interesting Three Continents Radio Shows. We would also like to extend a special thanks to Kehinde Andrews, Dulce Lempiainen, and Cheryl Payne for the sterling work undertaken in their discourse analysis of media coverage of Slave Trade Abolition in 2007, culminating in a presentation to our closing event at the Drum on 28th March 2008.

In helping us to fulfil our objective of engaging young people in their history, Three Continents, One History would like to thank Aston Manor School, and Jenny Bartley and Tamar Francis in particular, for co-ordinating and delivering the dramatisation workshops involving Year 7 and Year 8 pupils.

As the project moved towards its conclusion, other individuals and organisations played their part. For the permission and assistance rendered in the use of images from their respective collections, the project would like to thank the following: Birmingham Archives & Heritage; Leif Svalesen from the UNESCO Slave Routes Fredensborg project; the British Library - Images Online; Birmingham Museums & Art Gallery; Staffordshire Regiment Museum; The Royal Regiment of Fusiliers in Warwick; Worcestershire Regiment Museum; Galen Frysinger, and John Todd Jr.

As is often the case in any project, particular individuals have stood out in the support and encouragement that they have offered. Into this special category we would like to place Dr Andy Green (Birmingham Archives & Heritage) for his patient and unflagging support of, and contribution to, the project. Andy has been there from start to finish. In helping us to conceive, research and realise the project, he has rendered invaluable assistance. Latterly, our book designer, Simon Meddings, has worked with us patiently to help us realise an output that will do justice to the hard work and commitment of all those who have contributed to the project. This book itself was not originally one of our projected outputs. It is to Carey Burke that we should give thanks for seeing the necessity of translating the constant requests for information from our audiences into a publication that would leave a lasting legacy for the project.

Without the significant support of the Heritage Lottery Fund (HLF), there would have been no Three Continents, One History Project. In recognition of this support, we would like to extend our thanks to all those at HLF who have believed in and kept faith with, what we consider to be a worthy contribution to the events of 2007. Particular thanks must go to our project monitor, Sita Ramamurthy, who has worked with the project from start to finish. Under her guidance and constructive support, the project has been able to move from the structuring of an idea to the delivery of real outputs.

Last, but not least, we would like to thank all those who have participated in the Three Continents, One History events and listened to our Three Continents Radio Shows. To the presenters who participated in our events and radio shows, we would like to extend our appreciation for sharing with us and our audience your knowledge.

Right: Bance Island, ca.1805. One of the main trading forts/factories established by the British (Royal African Company) in 1672 for processing African captives. The factory included a 'great house' for the Chief Agent, quarters for captives, officials and soldiers, a jetty and a fortification with 16 cannons. Joseph Corry, *Observations upon the Widward Coast*, British Library Board. All rights reserved 072808.

BANCE ISLAND, in the RIVER SIERRA LEONE.
The Property of John & Alexander Anderson Esq.rs London.

Three Continents, One History Project Team

Dr Clive Harris, Project Director/Lead Researcher
Carey Burke, Project Co-ordinator
Dr Rebecca Condron, Researcher
Sophia 'Ankhobia' Carvalho, Lead Broadcaster/Researcher
Ebony Matthews, Broadcaster/Researcher

If you would like to contact the Three Continents, One History Project, please visit our website at www.threecontinents.co.uk.
or email: info@threecontinents.co.uk

We appreciate any comments you may have about this book or our project website.

acmc

Afro-Caribbean Millennium Centre
339 Dudley Road, Winson Green, Birmingham B18 4HB
www.threecontinents.co.uk

Joseph Ignace • Jozef Caridad Gonzalez • Juan de Bolas • Julien Fedon • King Tackey • King Zumbi • Kwame Nkrumah • Leonard Howell • Lobby • Louis Delgres • Lucas Dantas • Luis Gonzaga • Luisa Mahin • Mackandal • Malcolm X • Manikongo Afonso (Mvemba Nzinga) • Manoel Congo • Manuel Balaio • Manuel Faustino • Marcus Mosiah Garvey • Martin Luther King • Mary Prince • Mary Seacole • Nanny of the Maroons • Nat Turner • Nelson Mandela • Olaudah Equiano • Otto Huiswood • Ottobah Cugoano • Patrice Lumumba • Paul Bogle • Paul Cuffe • Peter Tosh • Phibbah • Phyllis Wheatley • Prophetess Kimpa Vita • Preto Cosme • Queen Nzinga • Rosa Parks • Samuel Coleridge-Taylor • Samuel 'Daddy' Sharpe • Sandy • Santa Eufrasia • Sengbe Pieh (Joseph Cinque) • Sojourner Truth • Solitude • Steve Biko • Stokeley Carmichael (Kwame Toure) • Teresa de Benguela • Tubal Uriah Butler • Tula • W.A. Domingo • Walter Rodney • W.E. Dubois • Winnie Mandela • Yaa Asantewaa • Yosef Ben Jochanan • Zeferina • Zumbi •

...and many more unsung freedom fighters whose names do not appear